THE TRIAL *of* LEVI WEEKS

THE TRIAL *of* LEVI WEEKS

ALEXANDER HAMILTON, AARON BURR, AND THE FIRST RECORDED MURDER TRIAL IN US HISTORY

ESTELLE FOX KLEIGER

CHICAGO REVIEW PRESS

First published in 1989 by Academy Chicago Publishers
This edition published in 2025 by
Chicago Review Press Incorporated
814 North Franklin Street
Chicago, Illinois 60610
ISBN 978-0-89733-997-1

The Library of Congress has cataloged the first edition as follows:
Kleiger, Estelle
The trial of Levi Weeks/ by Estelle Kleiger.
p. cm.
Bibliography: p.
ISBN 0-89733-492-2
ISBN-13 978-0-89733-492-1
1. Weeks, Levi—Trials, litigation, etc. 2. Trials (Murder)—New York (N.Y.) I. Title.
KF223.W44K.59 1989
345.73 '02523—dc19 87-37370
[347.3052523] CIP

Cover design: Preston Pisellini
Cover images: (clockwise from upper left) Aaron Burr; Alexander Hamilton; Federal Hall, New York City, circa 1790; uncolorized originals courtesy of the Library of Congress Prints and Photographs Division

Printed in the United States of America

For Miriam and Richard and Marjorie
and Bea and Sarah and Aaron

CONTENTS

Foreword

During the autumn of 1819 a relatively young (forty-three) but highly respected local architect died in Natchez, Mississippi. A marker for Levi Hinckley Weeks, to be found in the Natchez City Cemetery, identifies him as having been the "Architect of Auburn" and gives his relevant places and dates, noting that he was born October 22, 1776, in Greenwich, Massachusetts, and died in Natchez on September 20, 1819.[1]

There is no hint here of the notorious New York murder trial that had made Weeks infamous throughout the Eastern Seaboard nearly twenty years before his death. All we have is mention of his most splendid architectural accomplishment: the opulent Natchez mansion known as Auburn, which still stands today as a testament to his undeniable talent.[2]

In our modern era we have become inured to the phrase "trial of the century." Think about how often such trials occurred during the twentieth century. Leopold and Loeb, Sacco and Vanzetti, the Lindbergh kidnapper, Charles Manson, Ted Bundy, O. J. Simpson—at one time or another each of these cases, and others besides, were identified as being far more astonishing and spectacular than all of the century's previous homicide-related judicial proceedings.

But the murder trial of Levi Weeks—broadly publicized in 1800, the very last year of the eighteenth century—truly *does* appear to have been *the* trial of that century. Occurring on the evening of December 22, 1799, on the heels of the December 14 death of George Washington, what came to be called the Manhattan Well Murder not only capped off the 1700s and the revolutionary era that defined them but also led to the very first recorded murder trial in the history of the American Republic.

The ingredients for scandal and outrage were there from the start. The victim was a presumably pure and naive young woman—twenty-one-year-old Gulielma "Elma" Sands—lured from her cousin's boardinghouse on Manhattan's Greenwich Street and killed in the dark of a frigid evening. The most likely suspect: her rumored lover (and fellow boarder) Levi Weeks, whom, according to the testimony of her cousin and landlady, Catherine Ring, Sands had thought she'd be marrying the very night of the murder.

Add to this the gruesome finding of the body down a well located amid a long-lost Manhattan wetland called Lispenard Meadows in what is now SoHo.[3] The bruised and hideously soggy corpse, which had apparently been beaten and strangled, invited the attention of a public always fascinated by the grotesque. And there was plenty of grotesque to be had, as when Sands's cousin displayed her in her coffin on the street outside the boardinghouse. Hundreds came to bear witness.[4]

A woman betrayed. A despicable adventurer. The stuff of a novel. And the stuff of a trial that promised much in the way of drama.

With a population of about sixty thousand, Manhattan was nevertheless still a small place at least when it came to its leading citizens: prominent bankers, landowners, merchants, attorneys, politicians, court magistrates, and builders. These elites, the equivalent of today's top 1 percent, socialized and otherwise convened within a relatively tight circle. Instead of six degrees of separation, at that time the upper class of Manhattan society operated on a factor of two or three degrees at most. The surnames of these players can readily be seen on street maps of modern Manhattan, Brooklyn, and The Bronx—Lenox, Varick, Jay, Morris, and Livingston among them.

The accused murderer, twenty-four-year-old Weeks—at that time employed as a carpenter—had his own wealthy connections, despite his residence in a modest boardinghouse where he shared a room with his apprentice. Weeks's older brother Ezra was a prominent builder and friend of Aaron Burr (for whose Manhattan Company—a real estate development firm—Ezra had done extensive work).[5]

At the time of the murder, Ezra and his frequent partner, architect John McComb Jr., had recently finished building what is now known as Gracie Mansion—today the official residence for mayors of New York City. (It is likely that Levi participated in the construction of Gracie Mansion.) Ezra and John would in the next couple of years be involved in constructing the home to be called The Grange, commissioned by Alexander Hamilton for himself and his family.

It was Ezra, apparently, who with his wealth and connections managed to lure from the incestuous upper ranks of New York society three of the city's most prominent attorneys and enlist them in the defense of his brother against conviction for capital murder. Two of them, Alexander Hamilton (a Federalist) and Aaron

Burr (a Democratic-Republican), were fierce political rivals who nevertheless—at this point, at least—remained somewhat cordial. (At the time, no one could have foreseen the 1804 duel on the banks of the Hudson at Weehawken, New Jersey, that would leave Hamilton dead and Burr despised to the point that he soon had to resign his position as the Democratic-Republican Thomas Jefferson's vice-president.)

A third attorney, Democratic-Republican (Henry) Brockholst Livingston—who had dropped his first name—brought the most distinguished of pedigrees to the team. A scion of the famed baronial landholding family of Livingston Manor in Upstate New York, he was the son of William Livingston, the first governor of New Jersey. The elder Livingston also represented that state in the Continental Congress and was a signer of the Constitution, and Brockholst himself would go on to become an associate justice of the US Supreme Court in 1806, during the presidency of the Thomas Jefferson.[6] (As if to qualify for the Weeks defense team, Livingston in 1798 had killed one James Jones in a duel on the same Weehawken beach where Burr would later kill Hamilton.)

In short, the conglomeration of prestigious defense attorneys made the judicial proceedings in the Sands murder even more newsworthy than it might have been otherwise.

In *The Trial of Levi Weeks,* author Estelle Fox Kleiger does a superb job of chronicling and analyzing the courtroom proceedings.[7] At the time of its first publication, the book received glowing reviews in *The Wall Street Journal, The New York Times,* and numerous other newspapers and journals. Here Kleiger presents the full transcript of the trial—the first American trial to be thus recorded—and illuminates this transcript with invaluable insights gleaned from her extensive research around not only the trial but also the social and political environment in which it transpired.

As Kleiger eloquently shows, throughout the often-tumultuous proceedings, Levi Weeks's defense team did a good job of sowing reasonable doubt as to their client's guilt. They did so through a variety of approaches—one of them being to question the timeline of Weeks's documented appearances at other city locales during the presumed period of the murder.

Not stopping there, they presented information that did much to cast suspicion on another resident of the boardinghouse: Richard Croucher, an Englishman who had been in the United States but a few months, who they implied had enjoyed intimate relations with Sands. (Croucher, it should be noted, had been among the first and loudest to publicly accuse Weeks of the crime, and enthusiastically testified against him during the trial.)

As something of a coup de grâce, the defense attorneys closed the deal with a tactic still popular today. They put the victim on trial, portraying Sands as a loose woman who, they suggested, had been intimate with not only Croucher but also others—including her cousin's husband, Elias Ring—and who was a chronic abuser of the drug laudanum.

Today no one can know for sure whether Weeks was actually guilty—or Croucher, for that matter. However, some facts are worth noting. As we know, Weeks went on to live an honorable, blameless, and prosperous life. Not so with Croucher. Within weeks of the trial's conclusion, Croucher found himself convicted and sentenced to life in prison for raping a thirteen-year-old girl. Following the receipt of a pardon (arranged a few years later by his attorney Brockholst Livingston) he was subsequently indicted for fraud in Virginia, whereupon he absconded to his native Britian before sentencing. There he was later executed for what one of Alexander Hamilton's sons would describe as "a heinous crime," most likely murder.[8]

Yet popular belief throughout Manhattan largely continued to condemn Weeks and disparage him as a wanton and unrepentant killer. This was, one assumes, the reasoning behind his leaving town and his eventual journey to the South—where, according to at least one historian, his arrival can be marked as "perhaps the most important event in the architectural development of Natchez."[9]

Perhaps it is for this that he should best be remembered.

EDWARD J. RENEHAN JR.
NEWPORT, RHODE ISLAND

NOTES ON THE FOREWORD

[1]The Auburn Garden Club installed the marker some twenty years ago. It is located near the grave of Lyman Harding, who commissioned the building of the mansion Auburn in 1812, and not far from the presumed gravesite of Levi Weeks. Auburn—located at 400 Duncan Avenue, Natchez—is today a period museum open to the public.

[2]Natchez structures attributed to Weeks include not just Auburn but also Mercer House, 118 South Wall Street (built in 1817), and the East Wing of Jefferson College.

[3]The location of the well was most likely at the rear of the property that is today 89 Greene Street. (See Henry Mills Alden, ed., *Harper's New Monthly Magazine* 44 [1872]: 924.) The well's

remains have never been found nor, evidently, sought to any great extent. During the late twentieth century, the owners of a trendy SoHo restaurant called the Manhattan Bistro, located at 129 Spring Street, just off the corner of Greene Street, decided to expand their wine cellar. When workers broke through a basement wall, they discovered what some assumed to be the infamous well—a large circular shaft of stacked and mortared brick. This, however, is far more likely the remains of a cistern belonging to William Dawes, who in 1817 commissioned the building of the Spring Street structure. Both addresses rest on land that had been filled (circa 1811) atop the old Lispenard Meadows wetland. NOTE: The land is also referred to in different sources as Lispenard's Meadows, Lispenard Meadow, and Lispenard's Meadow. The last variation probably describes the site most accurately, as there was only one meadow, originally owned by a man named Lispenard. In keeping with that, several witnesses during the trial referred to "Lispenard's," according to the transcript. ALSO NOTE: Some sources identify these addresses as being located in today's Tribeca. In fact, they are in the adjacent SoHo neighborhood.

[4]The Ring and Sands families were Quaker, so the Rings had Sands buried in the Quaker cemetery on the south side of East Houston Street between Bowery and Chrystie, in what is now Manhattan's Bowery Historic District. All interments at this cemetery were, decades later, removed variously to a new Quaker cemetery within the borders of what is today Brooklyn's Prospect Park and to the cemetery of the Westbury Friends Meeting House on Long Island. In which location Sands eventually wound up cannot be guessed.

[5]Ezra Weeks, born in Massachusetts in 1772, spent the bulk of his adult life living in Manhattan, where he died in 1849. His principal residence throughout those years was 12 Leroy Place in Greenwich Village—Leroy Place being at the time one of the most prestigious and expensive developments in the city, located on Bleecker Street between Mercer and Greene Streets. No trace of Leroy Place remains today. NOTE: The location of Ezra's grave is unknown.

[6]In her text Estelle Kleiger says 1807, but Jefferson actually named Livingston to the Supreme Court via a recess appointment

in 1806. His appointment became permanent when he was approved by the Senate the following year.

[7]Kleiger died February 5, 2017, at the age of one hundred.

[8]Robert and Marilyn Aitken, *Law Makers, Law Breakers, and Uncommon Trials* (New York: American Bar Association, 2007), 130.

[9]Patti Carr Black, *Art in Mississippi, 1720-1889* (Jackson: University Press of Mississippi, 1998), 35.

ACKNOWLEDGMENTS

My thanks to many New York City and Westchester librarians for assistance in ferreting out the material in these pages. Access to the wonderful collection of documents at the New-York Historical Society Library was achieved through the efforts of Marion Touba and Mary Cary, among many others. Westchester County's excellent library and information system made it possible for me to discover where in the county I might obtain certain works. It also gave me the privilege of working at Westchester college and university libraries. I am very grateful for the help of Janet Dempsey, Cornwall Town Historian, and Elizabeth H. Moger, Keeper of the Records at the Haviland Records Room. Special thanks go to Miriam L. Kleiger and Beatrice Fox for their help.

I would also like to thank Anita Miller for her editorial guidance, and Jane Kohen Winter of Academy Chicago Publishers who, on a trip to Natchez, Mississippi, discovered Levi Weeks's second life and who helped pull it all together, and the following Mississippians for contributing to the Natchez section of the book: Hunter Cole of the University Press of Mississippi; Hank Holmes and Michael Hennen of the Mississippi Department of Archives and History; Ron Miller of the Natchez National Historical Park Foundation; Edna Joseph of the Auburn Garden Club; Kathy Wesley of the Judge George W. Armstrong Library; David Gleason, photographer; Ronnie James; Sara McGehee; and the women who run Stanton Hall.

CHAPTER ONE

THE DISAPPEARANCE

On Sunday, December 22, 1799, shortly after eight o'clock in the evening, a young woman named Gulielma Sands left the boardinghouse where she lived on Greenwich Street in New York City; she was never to return alive. After a day or so, when it became apparent that Elma, as she was called, had not spent the night with friends, Catherine and Elias Ring, who owned the boardinghouse, became apprehensive about her welfare. A search was mounted for Elma; as the days passed apprehension turned to dread.

A week after her disappearance, some boys playing in Lispenard Meadows found Elma's borrowed muff floating in the Manhattan Well—so called because it had been dug by Aaron Burr's Manhattan Company. The Well was probed and Elma's bruised and sodden body was fished from its depths.

Catherine Ring was Elma's cousin; she and her husband Elias were Quakers. They lived with their four children and Catherine's sister, Hope Sands, in the boardinghouse at 208 Greenwich Street; Elma had been with them for three years. The New York City Directory for 1798 lists Elias Ring as having a dry goods store at that address.

In those days, when there were no defined "shopping areas" in the city, merchants frequently ran businesses in their homes. In fact, Catherine Ring ran a millinery shop at 208 Greenwich Street; it was a good-sized enterprise which employed as many as twenty young women, including Elma Sands. At the neighboring house on one side of the Rings, Lorena and David Forrest lived and sold tobacco. On the other side was the house of Joseph Watkins, an ironmonger. Watkins' house furnishing store and nail factory was a well-known and thriving establishment.

In 1776, while the British occupied New York, fire destroyed 1,000 buildings; in 1778 there was another disastrous conflagration. Because of this and because the population of the city was growing rapidly—it was 30,000 in 1789 and 60,000 ten years later—there was a housing shortage. Newcomers to the city, whatever their class and financial situation, usually stayed in boardinghouses until they could find permanent housing. In 1789 there were said to be 330 boardinghouses in New York City, many of them quite elegant, but all of them filled to capacity.[1]

At the time of Elma's disappearance there were five boarders unrelated to the Rings at the Ring house, and a lodger who did not take his meals there. One boarder was a young woman named Margaret Clark; the others were men, among them a young carpenter named Levi Weeks who shared his room with his apprentice. On the Sunday evening she disappeared, Elma had confided to Catherine Ring that she and Levi Weeks were to be secretly married that night. Thus suspicion immediately fell on Levi Weeks.

On January 4, 1800, the *New York Daily Advertiser* printed the story:

> Thursday afternoon the body of a young woman by the name of Gulielma Elmore [sic] Sands, was found dead in a Well recently dug by the Manhattan Company, a little east of Mr Tyler's. The circumstances attending her death are somewhat singular—She went from her uncle's [sic] house in Greenwich Street last Sunday evening with her lover, with an intention of going to be married from which time until yesterday afternoon she had not been heard of. Strong suspicions are entertained that she has been wilfully murdered.[2]

Although the newspaper was filled with details of national mourning for George Washington, who had died on December 14, 1799, this item attracted a good deal of attention. It was the nature of this crime that upset the citizens; the city of New York, with a population in 1800 of 60,515, was not free from random murder. A period of lawlessness had followed the Revolution and the watch had been increased: no protection was provided during the day, but at ten o'clock each night the watchman collected his lantern, stick, rattle and badge, and started on his rounds wearing his "leathern hat" which had earned him the nickname of "leather head." These men often dozed off in their watchboxes, because most of them had to work full-time jobs during the day to augment their skimpy salaries. There is a story about the young Washington Irving and his friends throwing a rope around an occupied watchbox and towing it down the street while the rudely awakened watchman protested loudly from inside it.

"The number of crimes is greater in the city of New York than elsewhere in the state," wrote a European visitor. "In the city there is one crime for every 129 persons. In the state, one for every 2633."[3] And, indeed, although the jails were filled to capacity, vandalism, street robbery and personal attacks continued to occur in the city. The crime center was Canvas-town, a burned-out section lying towards the East River from Broad to Whitehall streets where the housetops were covered with canvas instead of roofs. It was "a resort of disreputable people;"[4] in 1784 the Mayor had recommended to the grand jury that something should be done about riots and disorder in Canvas-town, and in 1800 the area was still festering.

In the center of the city, on the site of the present City Hall, stood the gallows, designed for some reason to resemble a Chinese pagoda, and stocks and whipping posts were nearby. On the frequent occasions when these devices were put to use, spectators flocked to cheer or jeer or simply to watch. There were times when as many as six criminals were hanged in one day. They were not all accused of murder: until 1796 hanging crimes included first offense burglary, arson, housebreaking and forgery. The theft of the most trifling article could bring "thirty-nine lashes on the bare back." Women as well as men were subject to this punishment: one Sarah Crowdy is recorded to have received twenty lashes for petty larceny.[5] After 1796 there was some penal reform, and the death penalty was limited to treason, murder and theft from churches. Flogging however was retained, left to the discretion of the court.

So crime was not a rarity in the city, and neither was violence: the upper classes committed their special violence against each other through duelling, which was illegal but very much a part of the social code, because only gentlemen duelled. The conviction of a duellist in a court of law was virtually unheard-of, and anyone who wanted to preserve his good name would not allow himself to be suspected of cowardice. He could not apologize to his adversary unless he were to learn that he had been unfairly critical of him. Disgrace was still the only alternative to the acceptance of a challenge, although many thoughtful people saw clearly that the practice was repellent. Alexander Hamilton once said, "We do not now live in the days of chivalry . . . The good sense of the present time has happily found out, that to prove your own innocence, or the malice of an accuser, the worst method you can take is to run him through the body or shoot him through the head."[6] Hamilton's son was killed in a duel. In 1804 Hamilton himself was challenged by Aaron Burr over a newspaper report that Hamilton had slandered Burr at a dinner party. Hamilton attempted to placate Burr by saying that his remarks had been in reference to political topics only, but Burr, unassuaged, had then demanded to know whether Hamilton had ever spread rumors that reflected on the Colonel's honor.

Unquestionably Burr knew that Hamilton had done so. Hamilton had written to James Bayard, that "this man Burr has no principle, public nor private;" that Burr was "without probity;" that he was a "voluptuary" with expensive tastes that could not be satistifed "by fair expedients."[7] Burr said later that the slanderous newspaper report had been the last straw; he could not "consistently with self-respect again forbear" from a challenge.[8] The result of course was death for Hamilton and disgrace for Burr. And the practice of duelling lost its glamor in America.

However, in 1800 duelling was still in its heyday, and, although Alexander Hamilton and Aaron Burr were hardly close friends, they were still on speaking terms. They often worked together on one side of a case, or on different sides of the same case. They were in fact to work together in the defense of Levi Weeks, against whom public opinion was enflamed. Gulielma Sands's death created a sensation in the city of New York: this was not a death for the sake of honor, nor was it the result of a drunken brawl in Canvas-town. A pretty young girl from a respectable home had been cruelly murdered, and rumors abounded that the young carpenter who lived in the Ring's boardinghouse had proposed marriage to her in order to enjoy her favors, and had then killed her to avoid keeping his promise. Handbills were distributed around the town implying Weeks's guilt, and the first newspaper accounts added fuel to the fire that threatened to consume the young man. It was said that Miss Sands had expected to be married on the night she died: "but alas," lamented the *New York Gazette and General Advertiser,* "little did she expect that the arrangements she had been making with so much care, instead of conveying her to the Temple of Hymen, would direct her to that bourne from which no traveller returns."[9]

The emotion of the people was exacerbated by the public display of Elma's body before the funeral; on the day of the funeral itself the crowds which came to view the body were too great to be contained in the Ring house. Consequently, the open coffin was displayed in the street, guarded against the surging multitude by friends and public officials.

Levi Weeks was arrested on January 2, when the discovery of the body was reported to the police. The coroner's inquest lasted from Friday morning, January 3, until the night of January fourth. Two days later, on January sixth, the *Commercial Advertiser* reported that "strong suspicions" which had arisen on the discovery of the body led to a coroner's verdict of "*murder* by some person or persons as yet unknown."[10] An indictment was quickly obtained against Levi Weeks and he was committed to the Bridewell to await trial. He was apparently released on bail because he was reported to have been taken up by the Sheriff on March 28, shortly before the beginning of the trial.[11]

At this point the attention of the newspapers turned from the tragic fate of the young woman to the serious plight of the accused man. The *New York Gazette* backed off from what it called an "improper construction" in its previous report: "It is not our wish to hold Levi Weeks up as guilty . . . We understand he has, contrary to former accounts, universal testimony in favor of his character." It was believed by "respectable authority," the *Gazette* continued, "that the young man is innocent, or that his guilt is at least extremely questionable . . . The Public are desired to suspend their opinion respecting the cause of the death of the young woman whose body was found lately in the Well [so that the prisoner] may be condemned or acquitted by the free and unprejudiced voice of an impartial jury."[12]

One might think that this cautionary note had been injected into the discussion of the affair to assure a fair trial. However, a strong concern for the rights of the accused in felony cases had not been a part of the process in the Colonies, and consequently was not to be taken for granted in the new Republic. Under English law, felonies had been considered the province of the king, and the law was weighted against the defendant and in favor of the prosecution, which in fact represented the Crown. For centuries the accused had no right to counsel; it was left to the presiding judge to decide whether to give him assistance. During the course of the eighteenth century, defendants were allowed to consult counsel on points of law if the judge gave permission, and if the prisoner knew that he could ask for such consultation; he was not automatically informed of this privilege. In England the right to counsel in felony trials was not granted until 1836, with the passage of the Prisoner's Counsel Act.

Courts and legislators in colonial New York modeled their attitudes toward those accused of felonies upon English law, and since few lawyers were allowed to give any counsel to defendants in criminal cases, only the prosecution—the Attorney General and his staff—had extensive experience in criminal law. Lawyers had little opportunity to glean experience from representing people accused of misdemeanors because, although these people had been granted the right to counsel, few could afford legal fees, and no financial assistance was given them by the court. Defendants had to pay court fees even if they were found to be innocent.

In 1777, the adoption of the Constitution introduced some reform of this situation: Article 34 provided that "in every trial . . . for crimes or misdemeanors, the party . . . indicted shall be allowed counsel, as in civil actions."[13] After the Revolution at the first session of the New York legislature, the hideous punishments which had been traditional for prisoners who "stood mute," refusing to testify, were abolished, and laws were enacted which provided that a "mute" prisoner should be considered to have entered a plea of not guilty. This was as far as the new Republican courts wished to go in reform of criminal law. In 1788, the state of New York undertook to pay the expenses of prosecutors and of witnesses for the prosecution, which of course further weighted the scales against the accused. Officially, nothing was done to provide prisoners with legal counsel, although state courts often chose to appoint counsel for prisoners.

So one can assume that the sudden concern of the press for Levi Weeks's legal rights arose from something more than a tradition of judicial fairness. One factor may have been an understandable desire to quash riotous demonstrations of public hostility against the indicted man; but another may have been the discovery that this young carpenter had some powerful friends.

It must be borne in mind that, despite the undoubted egalitarian convictions of some signers of the Declaration of Independence and the Constitution, the new Republic was a class-conscious society. There was, for instance, no universal male suffrage; the vote carried property qualifications. In colonial New York a free male had had to own property worth at least the equivalent of a hundred dollars in order to cast a vote for members of the Assembly. After the Revolution, the New York state constitution cut in half the property requirement for voting for assemblymen and extended suffrage to tenement dwellers who paid the equivalent of five dollars a year in rent. So the number of white males eligible to vote for assemblymen was doubled, but at the same time the requirement for voting for governor, lieutenant governor and state senators was raised to the possession of property worth $250, more than double what it had been under the Crown. Although New York was the only state that allowed direct, written-ballot election of the government by the people instead of through the legislature, assemblymen and state senators were elected by voice vote until 1787 when the written ballot became legal.[14]

Since land was cheap in the countryside, tenement dwellers could often vote at least for assemblymen. In addition there was the legal device of the tontine, by which a number of men could band together to purchase property, thus claiming sufficient worth to be allowed suffrage. In 1800 approximately two-thirds of the free men in New York City, including blacks, could vote.[15]

However, American class-consciousness was strong enough that an article could appear in a newspaper suggesting a tax on hoops both as a source of revenue and a deterrent to the aping of their betters by the lower classes.[16] Aristocrats ruled the country as they had before the Revolution; their powdered hair, rouged faces and brocaded waistcoats set them apart from the ordinary population. A foreign visitor wrote:

> The society of New York consists of three distinct classes. The first is composed of the constituted authorities, government officers, divines, lawyers and physicians of eminence, with the principal merchants and people of independent property. The second comprises the small merchants, retail dealers, clerks, subordinate officers of the government and members of the three professions. The third consists of the inferior orders of the people. The first of these associate together in a style of elegance and splendor little inferior to Europeans.[17]

The question arises as to how Levi Weeks, described in the indictment as a laborer—although he was actually a carpenter—boarding in a house owned by Quakers, who represented egalitarianism and plain living, could afford the services of such prominent attorneys as Alexander Hamilton, Aaron Burr and Brockholst Livingston. The answer lies in the fact that Levi was the brother of Ezra Weeks, a man with property and impressive connections.

Ezra Weeks was a successful builder who was soon to purchase the entire block on which stood the Tontine City Hotel, which boasted one of the earliest slate roofs in the city, and which was the place where many of New York's most important meetings and social functions were held. It was there in 1798 that Gilbert Stuart's portrait of George Washington had been exhibited to the public for the first time. In addition—or perhaps more importantly for our purposes—in 1800 Ezra Weeks was working with the architect John McComb to build The Grange, Alexander Hamilton's estate on Convent Avenue. This building, which is still standing, was completed in 1802. John McCombs, as well as Ezra Weeks, was to be a witness for the defense in the Levi Weeks trial.

Since New York society was so small and tight-knit, it is not surprising to note that Ezra Weeks had also had business dealings with Aaron Burr; he had supplied wood for pipes for the Manhattan Company water system, which owned, coincidentally, the Well in Lispenard Meadows in which Elma's body had been found.

CHAPTER TWO

THE MANHATTAN COMPANY

His family connections were not the only thing that enabled Levi Weeks to procure impressive defense lawyers. There was also the fact that in the spring of 1800, only a short time after the trial, a crucial election was coming up which was to decide the political complexion of New York, and, indeed, of the country, for years to come. Everyone was obsessed by politics. The months before the 1800 election were the most bitter, politically, in New York history. It was "an era of bad feeling," a congressman said, when "a Federalist could knock a Republican down in the streets and not be questioned about it."[18]

Aaron Burr was actively engaged in work for the Republican-Democratic party, as was Henry Brockholst Livingston, another lawyer from a prominent family who was to be the third member of Levi Weeks's defense team. Alexander Hamilton was working with equal dedication for the Federalist party. Burr's efforts were to result in an unexpected Republican victory: the Federalists would lose the New York legislature, and since the legislature named the presidential electors, and New York was a pivotal state, the consequence was Jefferson's election, with Burr as his vice-president.

Therefore, in March of 1800, it was obviously desirable

that these lawyer-politicians should be in the public eye, and where better than in a courtroom upon which the attention of New Yorkers was riveted?

Added to the factors of friendship, business association and politics was the not inconsiderable matter of money. Although these lawyers were prominent men they did not necessarily have cash at their disposal. The new Republic was still suffering a financial depression. Milton Lomask, Burr's biographer, points out that in 1787, Patrick Henry could not go to Philadelphia for the Constitutional Convention because he did not have the money; in 1789, George Washington had to borrow to travel to New York for his inauguration, and Peter R. Livingston, a first cousin of Brockholst Livingston, was for many years afraid to leave his house because of his creditors. Speculation in western lands had destroyed the fortunes of many financiers, including Robert Morris, who had helped to finance the American Revolution.[19] There is no record among Hamilton's papers of his being recompensed for his work for Levi Weeks, and he apparently did occasionally work *gratis*. However Hamilton's Cash Book was not carefully kept and the payment may simply not have been recorded.[20] There was a good deal of demand for commercial law in New York at that time, with the setting up of new businesses and various legal tangles resulting from confiscations during the Revolution; the tightly knit group of lawyers had all the work they could handle.

However, Burr and Hamilton always needed money. Hamilton was barely solvent when he died. Although Burr's annual income in 1800 was said to be about $10,000—a large amount then—he always lived extremely well, and speculated unwisely in land. In 1797 he was forced to sell his furnishings to raise cash, and in 1799 he had to mortgage Richmond Hill, his impressive house, for $3800. In 1800 Hamilton wrote a friend that with interest Burr probably owed his creditors about $80,000. Thus Burr, at least, needed the fees that Ezra Weeks could afford to pay. And Burr's machinations had already involved him to some extent with the Weeks case, since the Manhattan Well belonged to his Manhattan Company. Ostensibly, the company was founded to provide clean water to the city of New York.

And New York needed clean water. As early as the 1740s, a Swedish naturalist had reported that horses were refusing to drink the bad water in the city's wells. By 1782, Fresh Water Pond, the most important source of water for New York, was polluted, and only the Tea Water Pump, next door to the Old Punch House at No. 25 Chatham Street, was being used. Every morning peddlers filled 130 gallon barrels of water from the Tea Water Pump—so named because its water had been said to make the best tea—to be sold in the streets at a penny a gallon. But by 1782 the Pump was contaminated through the Collect, a marshy area behind it, where dirty linen was washed in the summer, and "all impure things center together and engender the worst of unwholesome productions."[21]

By 1798, the situation was so bad that many physicians blamed the catastrophic yellow fever epidemic of that year on bad water, although some believed that the cattle, pigs and dogs which freely roamed the streets were responsible. Fifteen hundred people died of yellow fever in New York in 1798. In September, a newspaper warned its readers that "persons carrying the dead are not permitted to walk on the sidewalks close to the houses."[22] Flight appeared to be the only preventive: the roads around the city were clogged with streams of frightened refugees, their vehicles piled high with boxes and household effects. Taxes were not collected and the city had to negotiate a loan of $5,000 to pay the watch, which was doubled because of looting and arson.

Consequently, in 1799, Burr, with strong support from Hamilton, was able to persuade the state legislature to stand behind the formation of the Manhattan Company, a private municipal waterworks. Buried in this bill was what has come to be known as the "surplus capital" or "bank clause":

"*And be it further enacted,* that it shall and may be lawful for the said Company to employ all such surplus capital as may belong or accrue to this said Company in the purchase of public or other stock or in any other monied transaction or operations not inconsistent with the constitution and laws of the state or of the United States, for the sole benefit of the Company."[23]

Thus the Manhattan Company was granted the unprecedented privilege of using its profits "to operate a bank, insurance office, real estate business, trading company, or all of them simultaneously."[24] In fact this was Burr's real purpose in setting up the company: to establish a bank, sanctioned by the state, which would be under Republican control, since New York's two existing banks—the Bank of New York, and the local branch of the Bank of the United States—had been organized by Hamilton and were both therefore Federalist. Burr needed a bank that could help Republicans, himself included. The water company was a perfect camouflage for his intentions, which, if they had been baldly stated, would certainly have been rejected by the Federalists.

The legislature approved the bill establishing the Manhattan Company by a voice vote: Burr had placed some influential Federalists along with Republicans on the company's board of directors. No one questioned the bank clause. When the bill was brought for approval before the Council of Revision, the last step required by the state constitution before the governor signed it into law, only John Lansing, chief justice of the New York supreme court, objected to the clause. He was ignored. Chancellor Livingston had an option on 2000 shares of the company's stock. John Jay, the governor, who was married to a Livingston, signed the Manhattan bill on April 2, 1799. Jay was said to agree with Justice Lansing about the surplus capital clause, but he raised no objection to it.

A committee was set up by the company to find a plan for the procurement of water that would satisfy everybody. Some people wanted the Bronx River to be the source of the water; others said the River was too far away. "An aqueduct twelve miles long . . . is liable to twelve times the accidents of one mile," said the *Commercial Advertiser* in an editorial.[25] Elias Ring, who was on the committee, protested the stigmatization of the Collect as "a filthy, stagnated pond"; he said the water of the Collect had been pronounced pure by the eminent Dr Samuel Bard; it was never "discolored, putrid or thick, except sometimes near the banks, where it receives the wash of the streets, and is rendered in some measure filthy by throwing dead carcasses into it."[26] Elias Ring recommended high banks and fences to correct these deficiencies.

The plan finally chosen was the cheapest and the easiest to construct. It made use of a well that had been dug before the Revolution, and specified several new wells—all of them, unfortunately, to be dug in the vicinity of the Collect. Water from wells fed by the Collect was to be poured into a reservoir on Chambers Street. It was suggested that iron pipes be used in the water system, but these were deemed unsatisfactory, partly because of cost, and wooden pipes were substituted, which were laid by Ezra Weeks, Levi Weeks's brother, a builder of some distinction. Disgruntled citizens called the Weeks pipes "bored logs . . . which could be called pipes only by courtesy."[27] In 1828 it became necessary to remove the wooden "pipes" and install iron ones.

So a complex of wells was dug in and near the Collect, including, of course, the fatal one in Lispenard Meadows, a pleasant place where New Yorkers liked to stroll on Sunday afternoons. Within a few months of the water company's formation, applications were accepted from citizens who wished water piped into their basements—a system of pumping water to upper floors was not effected for several years. By the summer of 1800 about six miles of pine pipes had been laid, and about 400 houses supplied with water at a moderate charge. Unfortunately the water was not pumped with any degree of regularity: the quantity available was always uncertain; those closest to the wells received less than those situated further downhill. And the system was constantly breaking down.

Water was furnished free to firefighters through a pipe that ran down the center of the street; the firemen removed plugs from this pipe and connected suction devices to it to draw out the water. This was the origin of the term "fire plug." When the fire was extinguished, the men replaced the plugs. But the plugs were not always conveniently placed. And the network of pipes did not grow with the city. This is understandable, since the waterworks were not the Manhattan Company's primary concern.

In 1842 the Croton River Aqueduct provided "pure and wholesome" water to the city, but in order to avoid losing its charter the Manhattan Company continued to pump water long after consumers stopped buying it. Finally in 1900 the company was legally relieved of its water-producing function.

The Manhattan Bank, however, was a far more successful operation. It opened to the public in September,

1799, under twelve directors, of whom nine, including Burr, were Republicans. Burr paid for his victory to some extent in the loss of his Assembly seat in the spring of 1799. His reputation was clouded by the murky issuance of the Manhattan Company charter. However, the Bank was most useful to him: when he stepped down from the board of directors to form another bank, his debit on the company's books was almost $65,000. Alexander Hamilton came to regret his involvement with the establishment of the company. Its principles, he said, were those of "a perfect monster," although he recognized that it was "a very convenient instrument of profit and influence."[28] And so it was: the Manhattan Bank exists today, after a merger with the Chase National Bank, as the Chase Manhattan Bank.

CHAPTER THREE

THE PLAYERS

On the morning of March 31, 1800, crowds milled about the City Hall, at the corner of Wall and Broad streets, where the trial of Levi Weeks was about to begin: the first trial for a widely publicized murder in the new Republic. Those streets had not been filled with such a press of humanity since the inauguration of George Washington eleven years before, when an eyewitness wrote "in the streets the throng was so dense that it seemed as if one might literally walk on the heads of the people."[29] At that time City Hall had been called Federal Hall. The oath had been administered to the new president on an open balcony, and when the ceremony ended a flag was hoisted on the Hall's cupola as a signal to the artillery at the Battery to begin its salute. The crowd cheered amid the pealing of bells and the boom of cannon.

Now in 1800 the crowds around the Hall were in an ugly mood. The *Commercial Advertiser* commented: "The vague reports which had been in circulation from the time of her body having been discovered, until the hour of the trial, had irritated the public mind in such a manner as to draw to the place of justice a larger concourse of people and rendered it somewhat difficult for the Court at first to proceed to business."[30]

James Hardie, who was to provide one of the three

transcripts of the trial, wrote, "The concourse of people was so great as never before witnessed on a similar occasion in New-York." He estimated that not even one quarter of the people seeking to attend the trial were successful in their attempt. The rest remained outside, jamming surrounding streets and shouting for revenge: "Hang him! Crucify him!" Their hair-raising cries could be clearly heard in the courtroom. "Murder," wrote Hardie, "is a crime of so atrocious a nature, and at the same time so seldom committed in the United States of America, that . . . we become eager to find out the wretch who should be so sunk in villainy . . ."[31]

The trial was held at a session of the Court of Oyer and Terminer and General Gaol Delivery. Inside the courtroom the crowds were so great that constables were ordered to clear the room of superfluous spectators. Three men recorded the events of the trial. The least valuable record, by "a Gentleman of the Bar," was published by Longworth within hours of the verdict. A somewhat fuller version was published by James Hardie, who had apparently, in 1786, been a tutor to Alexander Hamilton's son Philip. He had also been a teacher of languages at Columbia University, and had received honorary degrees from that institution in 1787 and 1790. Hardie did not know shorthand, and he did not have a good seat from which to view the trial.

The version of the trial considered most reliable—although it has some faults—was taken down in shorthand by William Coleman, who claimed to have filled six notebooks with the events of the trial. Coleman was clerk of the circuit court, a position he owed to the influence of Alexander Hamilton. In 1801, Hamilton was to help Coleman become editor of the new Federalist newspaper, the *New York Evening Post.* Coleman had come to New York from Greenfield, Massachusetts, to clerk for Aaron Burr—

an experience which he later described as one of the worst mistakes he ever made. He could not have been compatible with Burr since Coleman was a staunch Federalist and Burr, of course, a Republican. Despite his relationship with both Burr and Hamilton, Coleman neglected to identify which member of the defense team was speaking, except in a very few instances. The omission was typical of trial reporting of the time.

The presiding judge in the Weeks trial was John Lansing, chief justice of the New York supreme court who, it will be remembered, was the only member of the Council of Revision to object to the "bank clause" in the Manhattan Company charter. Judge Lansing had served in the Continental Congress and had withdrawn from the Constitutional Convention in Philadelphia in 1787 because he believed that it had overstepped its authority. The Court of Oyer and Terminer could be formed by the mayor, recorder and one or more aldermen, or any three of these, sitting with a justice of the state supreme court. Consequently Judge Lansing sat with the mayor of the city, Richard Varick; the city recorder, Richard Harison, and Robert Lenox, an alderman. Both Harison and Varick were experienced lawyers.

Richard Varick was the second mayor of New York City. He had been Benedict Arnold's aide during the Revolution and had been deeply shocked to discover Arnold's treason. He petitioned Washington to hold a court of inquiry to clear his name which he feared might have been smirched because of his proximity to Arnold. A nineteenth-century historian makes this odd comment about Richard Varick: "He is said to have reversed the human maxim of the common law, by presuming a person guilty, if accused, until his innocence is proved."[32]

Richard Harison had been appointed recorder in 1798. He had been a Loyalist during the Revolution, but when restrictions against Loyalists were lifted, his law practice burgeoned. He was often associated with Hamilton, whose friend he was, as well as with Burr and Brockholst Livingston.

Robert Lenox had been alderman from 1797 and was to serve again from 1800 to 1802. He was a wealthy man who had made excellent investments in New York City land, and who had a reputation for unswerving integrity.

The prosecutor in the Levi Weeks case was Assistant Attorney General Cadwallader David Colden, the grandson of Cadwallader Colden, a distinguished physician, botanist and historian of the Iroquois nation, who had been lieutenant governor of colonial New York. The elder Colden's daughter Jane, the prosecutor's aunt, was a famous botanist in her own right. Cadwallader David Colden was to become mayor of New York ten years after the trial of Levi Weeks and he was later elected to Congress. At the time of the trial he was only thirty-one years old. The three defense attorneys were all in their forties, Livingston and Hamilton having been born in 1757 and Burr in 1756.

Defense attorney Brockholst Livingston (who had dropped his Christian name of Henry) came from a very prominent New York-New Jersey family which had been founded in America by Robert Livingston, a Scotsman who had emigrated to Albany, New York, in 1673 at the age of nineteen. He had amassed a fortune there, largely through trade with Indians, and become a trusted advisor to colonial governors. It was he who administered the oath of office to George Washington. William Livingston, Brockholst's father, was a respected lawyer who moved to New Jersey and became the first post-Revolution governor of that state in 1777.

Brockholst Livingston had been educated at the College of New Jersey, later Princeton, in the same years as

Aaron Burr, and, like Hamilton and Burr, had fought in the Revolutionary War. In 1779 he had gone to Spain as private secretary to John Jay, his brother-in-law, and on his return journey in 1782 had been captured by the British and held for a short time. He had passed the New York bar in 1783 and became an ardent Jeffersonian Republican, writing a number of newspaper articles opposing Jay's Treaty. Two years after the Weeks trial he was to become a justice of the New York supreme court and in 1806 Jefferson was to appoint him to the United States Supreme Court, where he would serve for seventeen years. He was a respected lawyer and scholar, but "violent in his political feelings and conduct."[33]

Aaron Burr's family background was also distinguished: his grandfather was the Reverend Jonathan Edwards and his father had been one of the founders and the first governor of Princeton. At the time of the trial Burr had already served as attorney general of New York and United States senator; he had been made a colonel because of his war service and he retained that title all of his life. He was shortly to become vice-president of the United States. Burr was a lover of books, and his fine library included some volumes which were radical for the times, among them the work of William Godwin. Hamilton had once remarked to a friend that Burr "in some instances . . . had talked perfect Godwinism." Godwin's wife was Mary Wollstonecraft, the mother of Mary Shelley, and the author of *A Vindication of the Rights of Women.* Burr himself was sympathetic to women's rights, and educated his daughter Theodosia accordingly. One of his most prized possessions, which he kept till the end of his life, was a painting of Mary Wollstonecraft.

Hamilton did not come from a prestigious family; he had been born into poverty in the West Indies, and there has always been some question about his legitimacy. But he had come to New York and attended Columbia College—then King's College—in 1774. His marriage to the daughter of General Philip Schuyler had united him with one of New York's oldest and most respected families. During the Revolutionary War he had been both a captain of artillery and secretary and aide-de-camp to General Washington. He had been a member of the Continental Congress and had worked during the Constitutional Convention for ratification of the Constitution, making many important contributions to the *Federalist Papers.* He was a strong proponent of centralized power, desiring to strengthen the federal government at the expense of the states, and he became a prime mover of the Federalist Party.

From 1784 to 1800 Burr and Hamilton were in the same courtroom during nearly every important case at the New York bar. They were part of a tight-knit and impressive legal community of about fifty lawyers who began practice immediately after the Revolution, of whom it would later be said that "in the last years of the eighteenth century and the beginning of the nineteenth, the standing of the New York bar for learning, efficiency and character has never been exceeded, and perhaps not equalled in a later period."[34]

When Burr opened his office in New York, American law was a sort of open field: no cases had been reported in the thirteen states, there were no written decisions, no precedents upon which to rely. Burr remarked, "The law is whatever is boldly asserted and plausibly maintained."[35] Commercial law was expanding as new businesses were being started up every day. Hamilton and Burr were much in demand because of their flexibility and impressive backgrounds. Brockholst Livingston, although not as dynamic as they, was nearly their equal. Their cases varied widely in importance, ranging from, for Burr, a suit for the return of a stolen horse to the Weeks case, and a commercial law classic like *Le Gruen vs Gouveneur & Kemble,* an often-cited case heard in 1800: it involved the sale and export to Europe of 600 bales of cotton and 1,200 pounds of indigo by Gouveneur & Kemble as agents for Le Gruen. The claim was for $120,000. Hamilton, Burr and Richard Harison won for Le Gruen while Gouveneur Morris, Robert Troup and Brockholst Livingston represented Gouveneur & Kemble, the losing side.

Since, as we have seen, legal representation of accused persons was discouraged, these lawyers had relatively scanty experience in criminal cases. Their presence in the courtroom certainly heightened the already feverish public interest in the case of Levi Weeks.

Chapter Four

CASE FOR THE PROSECUTION

The trial began at ten a.m. on March 31. It was to continue with only one recess until the verdict was returned more than forty hours later at three o'clock in the morning on April 2.

The prisoner was escorted into the courtroom accompanied by a voluntary guard of citizens. The first order of business was the selection of the jury. Thirty-four jurors were called and answered to their names. Then the clerk addressed the prisoner:

"Levi Weeks, prisoner at the bar, hold up your right hand, and hearken to what is said to you.

"These good men who have been last called, and who do now appear, are those who are to pass between the People of the State of New-York and you, upon your trial of Life and Death: if, therefore, you will challenge them, or either of them, your time to challenge is as they come to the book to be sworn, and before they are sworn, and you will be heard."[36]

The clerk then called the jurors to come forward, and the first of them came up. He was told to put his hand upon the Bible and the clerk said, "Juror, look upon the prisoner. Prisoner, look upon the juror," after which he administered the jurors' oath:

"You shall well and truly try, and true deliverance make, between the People of the State of New-York and Levi Weeks, the prisoner at the bar, whom you shall have in charge, and a true verdict give according to evidence, so help you God."

As they were called, all the Quakers on the panel, except one, came up to the Court and asked to be excused because they had scruples of conscience which prevented them from sitting in judgment on a case of life or death, and they were excused. The defense challenged eleven jurors and the Court excused them. Assistant Attorney General Colden attempted to challenge another juror because he had heard that he had made some remarks inimical to the prosecution's case, but the Court did not believe his objection was sufficiently substantiated, and it was dropped.

Accordingly, twelve jurors were sworn: Garrit Storm, dock builder; Simon Schermerhorn, ship's chandler; Robert Lylburn, merchant; George Scriba, merchant; Richard Ellis, grocer; John Rathbone, merchant; William Wilson, merchant; William G. Miller, baker; Samuel Ward, merchant; William Walton, merchant; Jasper Ward, merchant; and James Hunt, measurer, the Quaker who did not ask to be excused.

The clerk then addressed the jury:

"Gentlemen of the jury, the prisoner at the bar stands indicted in the words following, to wit . . ." And he read the indictment aloud:

> The Jurors of the People of the State of New-York, in and for the city and county of New-York, on their Oath present, that LEVI WEEKS, late of the seventh ward, of the city of New-York, in the county of New-York,

labourer, not having the fear of God before his eyes, but being moved and seduced by the instigation of the devil, on the 22d day of December, in the year of our Lord 1799, with force and arms at the ward aforesaid, at the city and county aforesaid, in and upon one GULIELMA SANDS, in the Peace of God, and of the said people then and there being, feloniously, wilfully, and of his malice aforethought, did make an assault, and that the said Levi Weeks, then and there feloniously, wilfully, and of his malice aforethought, did take the said Gulielma Sands into both the hands of him the said Levi Weeks, and did then and there feloniously, wilfully, and of his malice aforethought, cast, throw, and push the said Gulielma Sands, into a certain Well there situate, wherein there then was a great quantity of water; by means of which said casting, throwing and pushing, of the said Gulielma Sands into the Well aforesaid, by the said Levi Weeks, in the form aforesaid, the said Gulielma Sands, in the Well aforesaid, with the water aforesaid, was then and there choaked, suffocated, and drowned; of which said choaking, suffocating, and drowning, the said Gulielma Sands, then and there instantly died. And so the Jurors aforesaid, upon their oath aforesaid, do say, that the said Levi Weeks, her the said Gulielma Sands in the manner and form aforesaid, feloniously, wilfully and of his malice aforethought, did then and there kill and murder, against the peace of the said People and their dignity:—And the Jurors aforesaid, on their oath aforesaid, do further present, That the said Levi Weeks, not having the fear of God before his eyes, but being moved and seduced by the instigation of the Devil, on the same twenty-second day of December, in the year of our Lord 1799, with force and arms, at the same seventh ward of the city of New-York, in the county of New-York aforesaid, in and upon Gulielma Sands, in the peace of God and of the said People, then and there being, feloniously, wilfully, and of his malice aforethought, did make an assault, and [sic] her the said Gulielma Sands, then and there feloniously, wilfully, and of his malice aforethought, did strike, beat, and kick, with his hands and feet, in and upon the head, breast, back, belly, sides, and other parts of the body of her, the said Gulielma Sands, and did then and there feloniously, wilfully, and of his malice aforethought cast, and throw the said Gulielma Sands, down unto and upon the ground, giving unto the said Gulielma Sands, then and there by the beating, striking, and kicking her, the said Gulielma Sands, in manner aforesaid, several mortal strokes, wounds, and bruises, in and upon the head, breast, back, belly, sides, and other parts of the body of her the said Gulielma Sands, of which said mortal wounds, strokes and bruises, the said Gulielma Sands then and there instantly died:—And so the Jurors aforesaid, upon their oath aforesaid, do say, that the said Levi Weeks, her the said Gulielma Sands, in manner and form aforesaid, then and there feloniously, wilfully, and of his malice aforethought,

> did kill and murder, against the Peace of the said People and their Dignity.

"Upon this indictment," the clerk continued, "the prisoner at the bar hath been arraigned, and on his arraignment hath pleaded not guilty, and is now to be tried by his country, which country you are; so that your charge is, gentlemen, to enquire whether the prisoner at the bar is guilty of the felony whereof he stands indicted, or is not guilty. So sit together and hear your evidence."

Assistant Attorney General Colden then rose for his opening address.

> In a cause which appears so greatly to have excited the public mind, in which the prisoner has thought it necessary for his defence, to employ so many advocates distinguished for their eloquence and abilities, so vastly my superiors in learning, experience and professional rank; it is not wonderful that I should rise to address you under the weight of embarrassments which such circumstances actually excite. But gentlemen, although the abilities enlisted on the respective sides of this cause are very unequal, I find consolation in the reflection, that our tasks are so also. While to my opponents it belongs as their duty to exert all their powerful talents in favour of the prisoner, as a public prosecutor, I think I ought to do no more than offer you in its proper order, all the testimony the case affords, draw from the witnesses which may be produced on either side all that they know, the truth, the whole truth, and nothing but the truth. If I had the power of enlisting the passions and biassing the judgment, which those

opposed to me possess, I should think it unjustifiable to exert it on such an occasion.

Levi Weeks, the prisoner at the bar, is indicted for the murder of Gulielma Sands. He is a young man of reputable connections, and for ought we know, till he was charged with this crime, of irreproachable character, nay of amiable and engaging manners, insomuch that he had gained the affections of those who are now to appear against him as witnesses on this trial for his life. These are circumstances greatly in his favour, and there is no reason to fear that they will not be urged with all their force. We are aware that you will not convict such a one of the horrid crime of which he is accused upon less than the utmost evidence that the nature of the case admits, and that you will not readily be convinced that one so young has already embrued his hands in the blood of the innocent.

The deceased was a young girl, who till her fatal acquaintance with the prisoner, was virtuous and modest, and it will be material for you to remark, always of a cheerful disposition, and lively manners, though of a delicate constitution. We expect to prove to you that the prisoner won her affections, and that her virtue fell a sacrifice to his assiduity; that after a long period of criminal intercourse between them, he deluded her from the house of her protector under a pretence of marrying her, and carried her away to a Well in the suburbs of this city, and there murdered her—*(Here the Assist. Att'y. Gen. suddenly stopped a few seconds, as if overpowered with his emotions.)*—

No wonder, gentlemen that my mind shudders at the picture here drawn, and requires a moment to recollect myself.

In order to enable you to direct your attention the better to the testimony that will be offered, I shall proceed to detail to you more particularly the proof which I expect will be made.

I will not say, gentlemen, what may be your verdict as to the prisoner, but I will venture to assert, that not one of you or any man who hears this cause, shall doubt that the unfortunate young creature who was found dead in the Manhattan Well, was most barbarously murdered.

Elias Ring, and Catherine his wife, keep a boarding-house in the upper part of Greenwich-street; the deceased was a distant relation of theirs who lived with them. Hope Sands, a sister of Mrs Ring, and Margaret Clark, lived in the same house. In July last, the prisoner was received into the house as a boarder. Upon his first coming, for about a month, he shewed some attention to Margaret Clark, but soon after was observed to attach himself in a very particular manner to the deceased. Their conduct soon led to suspicions in the family, that there was an improper intercourse between them. In the month of September, Mrs Ring fled from the fever, leaving the care of her house to her husband, and the deceased; and leaving in it also the prisoner and some other boarders. Mrs Ring remained out of town about six weeks, and in that time it is certain that the prisoner and the deceased lived together in the most intimate manner. On the first of December last, the deceased disclosed to Hope Sands, that on the next Sunday she was to be married to the prisoner, but at this time, and whenever afterwards she spoke on the subject, enjoined on Hope the strictest secrecy, forbidding her to tell even Mrs Ring, saying that Levi meant to keep their marriage a secret, even from her (Hope) and therefore that no one should go with them to see the ceremony performed.

Between this time and the time of her departure from the house, it will be seen, she frequently spoke of her approaching marriage, and always with cheerfulness and a lively pleasure. On Saturday, the 21st of December, the day before the fatal accident—Hope disclosed the secret to Mrs Ring, informing her, that Elma was to be married the next evening. On the Sunday about dinner-time, Mrs Ring discovered to the deceased, that she knew her intentions. The deceased, you will find, then confessed that she was to be married, and that the prisoner was to come for her that night at 8 o'clock. Mrs Ring pressed the deceased to be of the party—She said Levi would not consent, as he meant to keep his marriage a perfect secret from all. In the evening you will see, the deceased began to dress herself, in which Mrs Ring assisted her; the deceased appeared perfectly cheerful all this time, she put on her hat and shawl, and went to a neighbor's and borrowed a muff, which she promised to return in a little time. She also took up a pocket-handkerchief belonging to one of the boarders, saying she should not make use of it, and would return it before it was missed. You will have evidence that the prisoner had left the house of Mr Ring, about five o'clock in the afternoon, and that about eight o'clock in the evening the deceased stood leaning over the front door, looking out—that Mrs Ring desired her to come in, saying, she did not believe Levi would come, to which she answered, she did not fear, it was not yet eight, but she left the door and went in with Mrs Ring, and in a little time the prisoner returned, and came into the room where was Elias Ring, Mrs Ring, the deceased, and two boarders, by the names of Lacey and Russel. Mrs Ring set with them about five minutes, when she got up and went to the street-door, and leaned over it till Lacey and Russel went up-stairs to bed. She then left the street door, and as she does perfectly remember, shut it after her; she went into the room again, and was hardly seated when the deceased went upstairs; Mrs Ring immediately followed her, found her in her room above, pinned on the shawl for her, and after being with her not more than two minutes, left her in the room opposite the stairs, just on the point of coming down. Mrs Ring returned to the room below where the prisoner was; in about a minute he took up his hat, and as he opened the room-door to go out, Mrs Ring heard somebody come lightly down the stairs, and as she supposes, meet him at the bottom; she then heard two voices whispering at the foot of the stairs for about a minute, she then heard the street door open and immediately shut, she took a candle and went to the door to look after them but it was dark and so many people passing, that she could not distinguish any one. The street door you will find, opens with a great and remarkable noise, in consequence of its being out of order. Gentlemen, it will be necessary for you to pay particular attention to this part of the evidence, for if you do believe that the prisoner, at this time, went out of the house with the deceased—I do not see how he can be acquitted. After Mrs Ring shut the door, it was not again opened till the time when she supposes the prisoner and the deceased went out. We shall show you that there were no other persons in the house till ten or eleven o'clock, but Elias Ring, who remained in the common sitting room, and the two lodgers, Lacey and Russel, who we shall prove to you lodged together, and were not out of their lodging-room, from the time they went upstairs. From this time the deceased was never after seen till her corps was found in the Manhattan Well. She had the marks of great violence upon her, and great part of her cloaths were torn off.

We shall produce a number of witnesses, who, between the hours of 8 & 9 of the evening of the 22d of December, heard, from about the place of the Well, the voice of a female crying murder, and entreating for mercy. It will be shown to you, gentlemen, that there was the track of a single horse sleigh, which we shall prove that at some time between the Saturday night before, and Monday morning succeeding, must have come out of Greenwich-street, and passed in a very extraordinary manner near the brink of the Well; that the snow round the edge of the Well was much trodden, and that the sleigh after having made a curious turn or stop near the Well, must have passed on to the Broadway road, and, in coming into that, turned towards town.

We shall proceed to shew you, that on the evening after the 22d of December, soon after the deceased left her house, she was met a few hundred yards from her house in the way towards the road that leads to the Well, in company with two men. That a few hundred yards further on, and about the same time, a single horse sleigh was seen with two men and a woman in it; the horse of a dark colour and without bells, passing on towards the road or street which leads from Greenwich-street to the Well.

Our next testimony will be, to prove to you, that a number of young gentlemen riding for pleasure on the same evening, as they were coming into town, between 8 and 9 o'clock, on the Broadway road, when they were some distance nearer to the town than the place where the track of the one horse sleigh was discovered to have turned into the Broadway road, they were overtaken by a single horse sleigh, which passed them with the horse on a full gallop, and without bells; there were two men in it and the horse was dark coloured. We shall then show you that Mr Ezra Weeks, the brother of the prisoner, was the owner of a single sleigh, and a dark horse, and that the prisoner had access to it when he chose, and we shall produce to you such testimony, as we suppose will satisfy you that this horse and sleigh was taken out of the yard

> of Ezra Weeks, about 8 o'clock in the evening of the 22d of December, and was returned again into the yard in less than half an hour.
>
> You will see, gentlemen of the Jury, that we have only circumstantial evidence to offer to you in this case, and you must also perceive that from its nature it admits of no other. I shall, however, reserve my remarks upon this subject, for a future stage in the cause; and shall, without delaying you longer, proceed to call the witnesses.

One of the prisoner's counsel (and unfortunately none of the three reporters bothered to distinguish, except in a few instances, among the three lawyers for the defense) asked the Court for permission to take the testimony of Elizabeth Watkins who was now in an adjoining house on her husband Joseph Watkins' affadavit:

> Joseph Watkins, being duly sworn, doth depose and say, That Elizabeth Watkins, his wife, was brought to bed on the sixteenth day of March instant, and that she has been very unwell ever since, and still is so, and that she has never been down stairs since she was brought to bed, and that he verily believes it would very much endanger her health to attend court. And this deponent doth further say, That the said Elizabeth Watkins' breasts were very sore and festered. And further the deponent sayeth not.
>
> Joseph Watkins
>
> Sworn this 31st March, 1800, before me.
>
> John Lansing, Jun.

Mr Colden said that he would raise no objection to the taking of Mrs Watkins' testimony in another place, since it was obvious that her personal attendance was absolutely impossible. He went with Judge Lansing and General Hamilton to take her deposition. When they returned Catherine Ring, the prosecution's first witness, was called.

Mrs Ring was "affirmed"—Quakers were not required to take oaths—and the defense interrupted to ask that her husband, Elias Ring, should "withdraw out of hearing" during her testimony since he was a witness, too. The Court ordered his withdrawal, saying that the prisoner had a right to it if he requested it.

Catherine Ring then proceeded to give her testimony. She spoke at length and did not wait for questions from the prosecutor, as would be the case in trials now. At this time Catherine was twenty-seven years old, a fair-skinned woman with an oval face and a high forehead. Her light auburn hair was covered with a plain bonnet: Quakers dressed for the most part in greys, browns and dull greens, shunning bright colors and ornaments. A poet had once said that when he spoke before an audience of Quaker women, he felt as though he were addressing a group of chickadees. "Let decency, simplicity and utility be our motives," the Friends said, "and not conformity to the vain and changeable fashions of the world."[37] They wished to avoid any show of material wealth, some of them objecting even to the use of carpets in the home. "Better to clothe the poor," they said, "than to clothe the earth."[38] They attempted to avoid class distinctions in speech, dress or behavior. They spoke what they called "the plain language," saying "thee" instead of "you;" they did not use the habitual names of days and months because these were derived from the names of heathen gods. The days of the week and the months were referred to by number: Sunday was "first day," Monday "second day," and so on, and January was "first month," February "second month" in the same way.

Quakers refused to take oaths because they believed that was forbidden by the Scriptures. And they maintained that they did not need to take oaths, since their religion required them to tell the truth at all times. They took this requirement very seriously and were widely respected because of it. In fact, the Manhattan Company stipulated that the board of directors must include at least two Quakers—presumably to keep the board honest.

Catherine Ring was the eldest daughter of David Sands, a Quaker preacher in Cornwall, New York; her wedding to Elias had been the first performed in Cornwall's new meeting house, providing an occasion for double celebration. The Rings had moved from Cornwall to New York only a few years earlier and had settled in the northern end of the city to be near the Quaker meeting house. So many Quakers were settling in that area that the local fire company had come to be known as "the Quakes."

Possibly because of nervousness, Catherine Ring named the month in which Levi came to live in the boardinghouse.

> *Catherine Ring:* In July last, Levi Weeks came to board in our family, soon after which he began to pay attention to Margaret Clark, till about the twenty-eighth of the eighth month, when she went into the country. About two days after her absence, Gulielma asked me—

The prisoner's counsel interrupted here to ask the opinion of the Court whether statements by the deceased were admissible as evidence; "this was a case of hear-say testimony," they contended, "and did not come within any of the exceptions in the book." They did admit that "the declarations of a deceased person were sometimes received as evidence against a prisoner, but it was only when they were made after the fatal blow, "in his last moments and when he must be supposed to be under an equal solemnity with that of an oath."

The Assistant Attorney General insisted that "such testimony was proper to show the disposition of mind in the deceased when she left the house on the night of the fatal accident; that this was the only way to discover whether she was sound in her intellects, or whether she was not under the impression of melancholy—and that in reality, this was one of those cases, where evidence was to be admitted upon the necessity of the thing." To support his argument he cited four State Trials.

Brockholst Livingston replied for the defense, denying that State Trials were any authority and citing authority of his own.

Colonel Burr repeated the defense position that hearsay evidence of the deceased could be admitted only when it was confined to "cases *in extremis,* after the fatal blow had been struck." He rejected the cases cited by Mr Colden, saying that in the first case no one had objected to the testimony and consequently no ruling had been made, and the second case had taken place in the court of sessions in Scotland and was therefore not valid as an authority in the United States.

The Court unanimously refused to admit the testimony. Although the trial had just begun, this was the second of Mr Colden's objections to be rejected; the first was his objection to a juror. Mrs Ring was told to proceed, but to "suppress whatever Elmore had said to her."

Catherine Ring: Elmore lived in our house with us three years, as our child. After Margaret Clark had gone into the country a few days, Levi became very attentive to Elmore, to whom I mentioned it, and she did not deny it. She and Levi were left together with my husband either the tenth or the eleventh of the ninth month.

Defense: Which room did Elma sleep in while you were in the country?

Catherine Ring: In the front room, second story.

Obviously, defense counsel were permitted to break in during prosecution testimony. The sojourn in the country to which Mrs Ring referred was taken in mid-September by her and her sister Hope and the Ring children in order to avoid the yellow fever epidemic of 1799. They went to the Sands's family home in Cornwall, New York.

Catherine Ring: After I had been absent about four weeks, I received a letter from my husband, desiring me to come home as he was very lonesome. I at first determined to return immediately, but I always thought Levi a man of honor, and that he did not intend to promise further than he intended to perform; therefore I stayed two weeks longer, and I came home six weeks to a day.

After my return I paid strict attention to their conduct, and saw an appearance of mutual attachment, but nothing improper, and always discovered sufficient in their countenance to convince me what was in agitation between them; and he was frequently in the room when she was sick. In a short time after my return, she concluded to pay a visit to her friends in the country, though she did not seem very anxious to go as it was so late in the season; however, after she got ready to go, Levi accompanied her to the vessel, and she stayed about two weeks.

During her indisposition he paid her the strictest attention, and spent several nights in the room, saying he did not like to leave her with Hope—my sister—fearing she might get to sleep and neglect her; and in the night he wanted to go for a physician, but I discouraged him, thinking she would get better by the morning. One night, after she had got much better, choosing to sleep alone, she went to bed; and as I suppose, Levi was gone also.

The prisoner's counsel interrupted at this point and informed the Court that Elias Ring, although he had been forbidden to remain in court, had come in again and was standing behind his wife while she was on the witness stand. The Court ordered the constable to remove him, and "reprimanded him for his behaviour." Mrs Ring resumed.

Catherine Ring: In about two hours I thought I would step up into her room and see how she did—I slipped off my shoes, and going quick without making much noise, I partly opened the door and saw him sitting by the side of her bed, and the door was shut against me—I took it to be by him, because she was in bed and could not reach the door.—The next morning he said he had made a fire just before day in his own room, and he discovered more concern than I expected.

Not a day passed but convinced me more and more that he was paying his attentions to her; I often found them sitting and standing together, and once in particular I found them sitting together on her bed. On the twenty-second of December, my sister Hope went to meeting, and Levi went to his brother's. In a short time he returned, having fallen and hurt his knee, which circumstance, it struck my mind, would prevent their intentions for that time.

Sylvanus Russel said, "Levi, you won't be able to go out today."

He answered, "I am determined to, tonight."

Elma then dressed his knee for him—it was not much of a hurt—I saw it—she got a plaister. After she had dressed it—he went upstairs a short time—she also followed him, and was gone, I should suppose, considerably more than an hour—this was about noon. His apprentice came down to do something, and in a little time went up, but soon returned again; the thought struck me that they had sent him down to get him out of the way.

Between twelve and one o'clock she came down into the room where I was preparing dinner, with a smiling countenance, and seemed much pleased. I spent the afternoon with her; her countenance and behaviour was calm and composed, and fully happy, as likewise her appetite remarkably good. I left her a short time and went into another room; when I returned I found Levi sitting by the fire with her, appearing fully composed and happy; but he soon left us and went upstairs. Shortly after Elma went also; in about twenty minutes she returned, not quite dressed, with her handkerchief in her hand, saying to me, "Which looks best?"

Then Levi came down, nearly dressed also, with his coat upon his arm, at which time Elma stepped behind the curtain of the bed.

He said, "Where's Elma?"

I said, "She is hid behind the bed."

He said, "Don't mind me—I want you to tie my hair."

Elma came out and did so. Elias came in from meeting and she went upstairs, and Levi after her; this was about sunset, and she did not come down till after dark, and Levi, I believe, stayed as long, for one of the family went up and found them together. I had got tea ready and waited some time for them to drink tea,[39] thinking they would drink tea together; but he did not come.

After tea I proposed borrowing a muff for her at one of our neighbor's—she said she would go herself, and she went and got it. A while after she went to the front door and leaned over it, which I soon observed. I told her I was afraid she would take cold; she followed me in, where was two young men of the family, Russel and Lacey, with my husband. We all sat together till Levi came in. I then went to the front door, and leaned over it. Soon after the young men came out and went upstairs to bed, at which time I heard the clock strike eight. After they had gone upstairs, I shut the door, and came in, saying, "The clock has just struck eight."

I sat down, and in the course of a minute or two after, Elma got up and went out, and I observed Levi's eyes fixed upon her, and I thought he looked at her for to go. In the course of about a minute, I believe not more, I took the candle and went upstairs. She had her hat and shawl on, and her muff in her hand. I observed she looked rather paler than usual, but I thought it a natural consequence, and I told her not to be frightened. I went down and left her just ready to follow. Levi took his hat—

Question by Defense: Pray how long was it from the time that Levi came in before Russel and Lacey went to bed?

Catherine Ring: About five minutes.

Defense: How long after Russel and Lacey were gone before you went up?

Catherine Ring: About one minute, perhaps.

Defense: How long might you remain there?

Catherine Ring: About a minute.

Defense: How long do you suppose it was from the time Levi came in, till they went out?

Catherine Ring: Elma might have remained in the room two minutes; in the whole I don't think all the time from Levi's coming in till they went out exceeded ten minutes.

Question by Mr Colden: Pray, Mrs Ring, in what situation did you leave Elma upstairs?

Catherine Ring: I left her just ready to come down, just coming down, she came down almost instantly. I came down and left her in the room and came in where Elias and Levi were sitting; no other person was in the house but we four. I set the candle down over the fireplace, Levi instantly took his hat and went out into the entry. The moment the door opened, I heard a walking on the stairs, and directly I heard a whispering near the door, at the bottom of the stairs for nearly a minute, but so near the door I thought I might understand what was said, and I listened for that purpose. Soon I heard them step along, and the front door opened, and the latch fell. I took up the candle and run to the door to see which way they went. It was moonlight but having a candle made it darker.

Question by Defense: Mrs Ring, are you sure you shut the door before?

Catherine Ring: I am positive. It stuck much, and it was difficult to shut it, it was something out of order, which made a jarring noise, and it stuck a good deal. I then run upstairs to see if she might not be there—why I did it, I don't know, I can't say, but somehow I felt agitated on the occasion. But she was not there.

Question by Mr Colden: Were the steps descending the stairs loud or not?

Catherine Ring: The steps coming down were loud.

Mr Colden: Did you or did you not hear the steps of one person only?

Catherine Ring: I heard the steps but of one person.

Here Mr Colden produced a plan of the inside of the house, and Mrs Ring was asked to explain it to the jury, which she did.

Mr Colden: How far is it from your room door to the front door?

Catherine Ring: About ten feet.

Mr Colden: What kind of staircase is it?

Catherine Ring: It is a hollow, close staircase.

Mr Colden: Would not a person coming down such make a considerable noise?

Catherine Ring: Any person certainly would.

Mr Colden: How near is your door to the stairs?

Catherine Ring: It is close to them; it opens against them.

Mr Colden: How far from the foot of the stairs to the outer door?

Catherine Ring: Not more than four feet.

Mr Colden: Are you sure about the sound of steps going out?

Catherine Ring: I am very positive; I heard the steps very distinctly.

Mr Colden: As to the steps on the stairs, how was it?

Catherine Ring: As he opened the door of our room, I heard the steps on the stairs.

Mr Colden: Could you not have been mistaken? Was there no noise in the room where you was?

Catherine Ring: There was no noise at all, nor anybody there but my husband.

Question by the Court: Did Levi return to his lodgings the same evening?

Catherine Ring: I was going to tell. About ten o'clock he returned, and his apprentice was there waiting for him as he had the key of the room, and the boy could not go to bed. The moment he opened the door I cast my eyes upon him, his countenance was pale and much agitated. His apprentice was standing waiting for him; he came to the fire, took the key out of his pocket and gave it to him, saying in a short tone, "Go to bed." He sat down and said, "Is Hope got home?"

I answered, "No."

"Is Elma gone to bed?"

I answered, "No—She is gone out, at least I saw her ready to go, and have good reason to think she went."

He said, "I'm surprised she should go out so late at night and alone."

I replied, "I've no reason to think she went alone," to which he made no reply, but looked earnest and thoughtful and leaned down his head on his hand in this manner.

She put her hand over her left eye, and leaned her head upon it.

Mr Colden: Had anything passed to lead him to believe that she went out alone?

Catherine Ring: No, there had not.

Question by the Court: Did you express any alarm to him?

Catherine Ring: No.—Feeling very uneasy and agitated, I thought I would speak to Levi more particularly than I had done, and I told Elias to go to bed, and I would fix* the child and bring it to him; and he got up to go, upon which Levi instantly rose and went upstairs. I thought she had gone to one of the neighbours to leave the muff; I was then determined to sit up until she should come in. I

*"Fix" here meant "dress;" Eliza, then the Ring's youngest child, had been born April 5, 1798.

accordingly put out the candle and covered up the fire, supposing that perhaps he would come down after he thought us a-bed, and let her in. After waiting till about twelve o'clock and nothing appearing, I lit the candle and searched the house, thinking perhaps that she had come in; and went to every room excepting that where the two lodgers was a-bed, and to Levi's room. I went to his door twice, but seemed as if I had not power to enter—I thought perhaps she might be sitting by Levi's stove. I then went to bed, and my husband was much surprised at my conduct in sitting up and searching through the house. I thought perhaps she had stayed at Henry Clements'. The next morning the boarders breakfasted early, about daylight. As usual, Levi came to breakfast.

Question by the Court: Was anything said about Elma at breakfast, by anybody?

Catherine Ring: No, nobody mentioned her.

After he had been out awhile, I heard some person enter the house and run softly upstairs, and expected it was her, and intended to go and see; soon after which Levi came in, saying, "Is Elma got home?"

I answered, "I have not seen her." I felt provoked that he should ask where she was, and thought that at least he might be silent.

He then said, "I am surprised where she should be."

I answered, "I expect she is upstairs. I heard someone go up."

He replied, "It was me you heard."

I observed, "Thee went more softly than ever before, and I'm sure I thought it her step."

He immediately run upstairs and instantly returned, saying, "She is not in the second story."

I did not believe him, and went up myself. When I returned he was standing at the front door, but I don't recollect his saying anything when I said, "I'm surprised where she should be," but went away.

Some time after he came in again and said, "Is Elma returned?"

I answered no.

"Have you sent anywhere for her?"

I answered no.

He said, "Why have not you?"

I answered, "I did not think of sending, expecting her in every minute."

He said, "I am surprised at her going out so late and alone."

I said, "Indeed, Levi, to tell thee the truth, I believe she went with thee. She told me she was to, and I have good reason to think she did."

He looked surprised, and said, "If she had gone with me she would have come with me, and I never saw her after she left the room."

He then went out.

Question by the Court: Was there anything uncommon in his manner?

Catherine Ring: There was to be sure, more than I can express.

Question by Defense: Do you mean that this was after you expressed your surprise?

Catherine Ring: I had observed his looks fixed upon me before.

Question by the Court: Did you tell him of this, did you observe to him that there was a difference in his look?

Catherine Ring: I did not then.

In a short time after, the owner of the muff called for it, as Elma had promised to return it the night it was borrowed, or early the next morning; I told her I would send for it, and the girl should fetch it home as I expected Elma was at Henry Clements'. She answered she would sit with me, and sat down, during which time Levi came in and sat until the girl returned, saying, "Elma has not been there."

I was struck with astonishment. Although my uneasiness had been great, yet I fully expected she was there.

The person immediately said, "I guess she has gone to be married, and that made her borrow my muff."

I answered, "Married or not, I think it very ungenerous not to return it, and likewise to keep me in suspense and uneasiness." At which conversation

Levi gave no answer, but set with his head down and then he went out.

Soon after this my sister returned; in a short time after Levi returned she immediately attacked him, saying, "Where is Elma? I know thee knows, tell me ingenuously, for Caty is very uneasy, and says Elma told her she was going with thee and she is sure she did."

He looked surprised and said, "She told Caty so? Why, if she had went with me, she would have returned with me. I never saw her after she left the room, and am surprised you would think of my keeping you in suspense."

The day passed without much more being said, except my saying I had been to the door fifty times to look for her; he answered he had looked more than fifty times; he could not keep his eyes from the street.

The next day being Tuesday the twenty-fourth, after the boarders had breakfasted, none of the family up then but them and myself, they all went out excepting Levi who, feeling me much distressed, walked the room several times appearing much agitated, came to me, and taking hold of my arm, said, "Mrs Ring, don't grieve so, I am in hopes things will turn out better than you expect." To which I gave no answer, as I expected that he was then going to tell me the whole matter. He soon however took his hat and went away.

Nothing more was said until afternoon, when

myself and sister being so distressed, we determined to stand it no longer and we were about to send for him when he again came in, laid down his hat; but on seeing our agitation he turned round and was going out.

I then said, "Stop, Levi, this matter has become so serious, I can stand it no longer." I then said, "It certainly lays upon thee, therefore thee must make the best of thy way to get clear of it."

He said he was willing to give what satisfaction he could, being sorry to see us so distressed.

I said, "If it had been many a person that I should have even been willing for her to have, I would not have waited one hour before they should have given an account of her, but my confidence in thee was so great, and fearing too to make her trouble, as she was bound not to disclose it, is the reasons why I did not previously mention it."

I then proceeded: "On first day after twelve o'clock, she came downstairs after being with thee, and told me, that night at eight o'clock you were going to be married, that you did not go till eight o'clock on account of it's being froze."

I had not proceeded much further, if any, before he turned pale, trembled to a great degree, was much agitated, and began to cry—clasping his hands together—cried out, "I'm ruined—I'm ruined—I'm undone forever, unless she appears to clear me—my existence will be only a burden—I had rather die in credit than live under it."

Then he proceeded to clear himself, saying he never would attempt to marry without his brother's approbation.

I replied, "She told me thee had talked to him twice on the subject."

He said, "My brother can answer for himself."

Thus he proceeded until we were hardly able to support it, as our dependence as to her was entirely upon him, not having a thought short of his knowing where she was.

On Thursday, the twenty-sixth of December, about ten o'clock, Margaret Clark and her sister Deborah Clark being in the room with me, Levi came in. Seeing us much distressed, he sat down and endeavored to comfort and console us, saying, "Give her up, she is gone, no doubt, and all our grieving would do no good."

With an earnest look I turned to him, saying, "Levi, give me thy firm opinion from the bottom of thy heart, for I don't doubt thee has one; tell me the truth, what thee thinks has become of her."

He replied, "Mrs Ring, it is my firm belief she's now in eternity; it certainly is, therefore make yourself easy, for your mourning will never bring her back."

I answered, "Why does thee say so? What reason has thee to think it?"

"Why, from things I've heard her drop."

"What were they?" I asked.

"Why, I heard her say she wished she never had an existence."

I replied, "If thee recollects, I don't doubt thee has heard me say so; I acknowledge it's wrong, and have reproved her for it."

Question by Defense: Pray, Mrs Ring, did you say you had wished that you never had an existence?

Catherine Ring: Yes, I daresay I have—in this very case, I might say, "I wish I never had an existence to witness such a scene." I acknowledge it's wrong, but still I don't doubt I often said so.

After a moment she resumed her testimony.

Catherine Ring: I asked Levi, "What other reason has thee?"

"Why, I have heard her threaten, if she had laudanum,* she would swallow it."

"Why, Levi! How can thee say so? As it was always easy for her to get that, it don't bear the weight of a single straw with me, and the circumstance thee alludes to, I believe I was present as well as several others—" which he did not deny, nor mention any other time—which circumstance was this: my sister was unwell; the doctor had left a small phial with her, [Elma], and she had it in her hand, clapped up to her mouth.

He [Elias Ring? Levi?] said, "Elma, don't do so."

She replied, "I should not be afraid to drink it if full."

My husband answered, "Why, the foolish creature! It would kill thee."

*Laudanum was derived from opium and often prescribed for illnesses.

She answered, "I should not be afraid."

I thought she spoke not thinking, though she was used to taking large quantities when sick, [which] made her think light of it, but I supposed she did it only to tease him.

I frequently conversed with him [Levi] on the subject, always pointing out the impossibility of any other persons knowing it, all which he never resented. On the day of the procession he came to me, saying, "Mrs Ring, what objection have you to Hope's going with me to the alderman to say what she can in my favour?"

I answered, "Yes, very great objections, if I even believed thee innocent, which I have no reason to think, and it's publicly reported of thee, if she was even willing, which I'm sure she's not."

"Well, then let her go with my brother."

"Indeed, I've no choice in thee or thy brother; if the authorities call for her, she will answer, I daresay, to what's proper."

He then said, "Mrs Ring, you are not so much my friend as you have been?"

"Indeed, Levi, I shudder to think I ever indulged a favourable thought of thee."

A question was interjected here; it is impossible to tell whether it was by the defense, the prosecution or the Court.

How long was this before her death?

Catherine Ring: About three weeks. [It would seem

that the question referred to the laudanum incident; otherwise it makes no sense. Possibly Coleman or the printer put this question in the wrong place.]

Mr Colden: Pray, Mrs Ring, I wish you would be particular as to her temper and disposition on the twenty-second; pray, inform the Court and jury, was it composed that afternoon?

Catherine Ring: Very much so, I never saw her pleasanter in my life—she was more so than usual.

Mr Colden: What was her general temper of mind?

Catherine Ring: Very lively, open and free.

Mr Colden: Was it not more so, than is usual among Friends?

Catherine Ring: I always thought her disposition rather too gay for a Friend, and she altered her dress and behaviour to please me.

Mr Colden: Pray Madam, has she not always borne a good character, I mean that of a modest discreet girl?

Catherine Ring: Very much so; I have known her from an infant, but there are others that can speak of her, who had not that partiality for her that I had.[40]

Mr Colden: Let me ask you, would not the conduct between the prisoner and her have been esteemed improper, if it was not supposed they were soon to have been connected in marriage?

Catherine Ring: Yes.

Mr Colden: How old was she?

Catherine Ring: About five years younger than myself. She was about twenty-two at the time of her death.

Mr Colden: Was Elma one of the Friends?

Catherine Ring: She was not so, though we wished her to be.

Mr Colden: Pray what relation was she to you?

Catherine Ring: She is my father's sister's daughter.

Mr Colden: Had she parents living?

Catherine Ring: Her mother is alive at New-Cornwall. Her mother never was married. She took her mother's name of Sands; her father is in Charleston, South-Carolina.[41]

Mr Colden: When was the body found?

Catherine Ring: The twelfth day after she left our house, or the second of January.

Here Mr Colden's interrogation of the witness ended; it was now time for cross-examination by the defense counsel, who began by asking Mrs Ring: What was the character of Levi Weeks while he boarded in your house?

Catherine Ring: It was such as to gain the esteem of every one in the family.

Defense: Was not his moral conduct good?

Catherine Ring: I never saw anything amiss in it. I should call it very good.

Defense: Did you observe whether the prisoner after this affair of the twenty-second eat his meals as usual?

Catherine Ring: I believe he did.

Defense: Was Elma considered as an associate for yourself and family?

Catherine Ring: She was. I regarded her as a sister.

Defense: Did she walk out with your family ever?

Catherine Ring: Hope and Elma walked out together. They were associates.

Defense: Did Levi ever walk out with her?

Catherine Ring: No, not as I know of.

Defense: Did he ever walk out with your sister Hope?

Catherine Ring: He went once to a Charity Sermon with her, and Elma was to have gone too, but the going was wet, and she was not very well, and I would not suffer her to go.

Defense: What was the appearance of Elma, the day she went out, the twenty-second of December?

Catherine Ring: She looked rather paler than usual when I pinned on her handkerchief—It was her natural colour.

Defense: What was the state of Elma's health generally?

Catherine Ring: For about a year past she was at times rather unwell.

Defense: Had she any habitual illnesses?

Catherine Ring: She was much troubled with the cramp in her stomach.

Defense: Where was her usual lodging room?

Catherine Ring: In the front room. She at first slept in the third story before she went to the country, but for three weeks before her death, she slept in the back room in the second story.

Defense: Was it not next to Mr Watkins' bedroom?

Catherine Ring: It was next, I believe.

Defense: Was there any other female in the house, when you went to the country?

Catherine Ring: There was not.

Defense: Did you ever ask Levi whether he was engaged to Elma?

Catherine Ring: Never till Tuesday, after her death.

Defense: Nor said a word about it to him?

Catherine Ring: No.

Defense: Did Levi appear lame in consequence of the hurt in his knee, on the twenty-second?

Catherine Ring: I do not recollect.

Defense: Had you ever any reason to suspect that any other person but Levi had an improper intimacy with her?

Catherine Ring: Never.

Defense: Did you never say that Mr Weeks was a person of a kind disposition?

Catherine Ring: Very likely, for I always thought him so.

Defense: Did you never say that Levi was very attentive to your children or any in your family, when they were sick?

Catherine Ring: I never did. I could not, for none of my children ever was sick while he was in the house.

Question by Mr Colden: Do you know of what materials the wall between your house and Watkins' is composed?

Catherine Ring: I don't know.

This last question bore directly on the defense counsel's previous question about Elma's bedroom being next to the bedroom of Mr Watkins, and also on the defense question about whether there was any other female in the house beside Elma while Catherine was away in the country. Obviously the defense was driving at something in connection to Elma's bedroom, and Mr Colden may have had some idea about it.

Hope Sands was the next witness for the prosecution. She was asked if she had observed any intimacy between the prisoner and the deceased.

Hope Sands: The first time I knew them to be together in private, was about two weeks after I and Elma came to town. I then found Levi and Elma together in her bedroom. I was there with Elma when Levi came in, on which Elma gave me a hint. I immediately went out, he followed me to the door and shut it after me, and locked it.

I went downstairs, left my shoes at the bottom of them, and went softly up to listen if I could hear their conversation, but could not understand anything although I heard a whispering and stayed at the door a long time, more than an hour. Hearing some person come in below, I run down, where I found Dr Snedeker; on my coming into the room, Peggy Clark took the candle and went up to the room where Levi and Elma were. On finding the door locked, she returned, much surprised at finding it fast, and asked me if I knew who was there. I answered, "I will go and see."

She followed me up to the door. Finding it locked, we went into the next room, when the door was unlocked and Levi came out. I observed to Levi that he intended being very safe, having secured the door that Peggy could not gain admittance. He then said, "Where is Peggy?" and looked into the room—but she stepped behind the door, so that he did not see her. He then left us and went upstairs. There was no light in the room when I left them, neither when he came out—therefore I am positive they had not any. I then went in and found Elma sitting on the bed.

Question by Defense: Did you ever tell Mrs Ring of this?

Hope Sands: Yes, I told her the same evening.

On Monday, the next day after she was missing, about ten or eleven o'clock in the forenoon, I met Levi upstairs alone. I attacked him about her—he denied knowing anything of her, though from his looks I was confident he did. He soon began to use all possible means to convince me of his innocence. I replied it was hard to judge one I had so good an opinion of, but he was certainly the person who could give information of her if he chose. He said, "Do you think if I knew where she was, I would not tell you?"

The Sabbath evening after she was missing, he came to me saying, "Hope, if you can say anything in my favor, do it, for you can do me more good than any friend I have in the world to clear me; therefore, if you can say anything, do it before the body is found, as after it will do me no good. But if the body is found a good way off that will clear me, as I was not a sufficient time from my brother's to go far."

He then pressed me very hard to go to the Alderman's and see him. I refused, upon which he gave me a paper he had drawn, wishing me to sign it. The purport of the paper was, that he paid no more particular attention to Elma than to any other female in the house—that nothing had passed between them like courtship, or looking like marriage. I took it from him, saying I supposed I might read it, and left him without saying any more on the subject till the day of the procession. He then came to me saying, "Hope, will you accompany me to see the procession?"

I replied, "No—I have seen processions enough."

He then said, "Hope, don't you intend to sign that paper for me?"

I answered, "No," and drew it from my pocket. I then pointed out to him the inconsistency of my doing it, saying, "Levi, if I was to do it, thee knows it would be positive lies."

He said it [the paper] would be of no service to me, and reached out and took it from my hand, saying, "Will you go to the police with me?"

I answered, "No."

He said, "Will you go with my brother?"

I replied, "No; what better would it be to go and say it than to sign the paper?"

He then asked me if I would consult my sister upon it?

I still answered, "No," for I was sure she would not consent to any such thing, if I was ever so inclined myself, which I am very far from.

The defense counsel began the cross-examination.

Defense: Pray how long do you think it was, that Elma and Levi were locked up together at the time you mentioned?

Hope Sands: About an hour, I should think.

Defense: Was not Levi as particular to you as he was to Elma?

Hope Sands: No, he was not.

Defense: Was not Levi very much liked?

Hope Sands: He was, very much; all spoke well of him.

Defense: Did Levi ever walk out with Elma, or with you?

Hope Sands: He went once to the Museum* with me and Elma. He went once to church with me of an evening; Elma was to have gone, but she was sick. I never knew him walk out with her but that time; I heard him say one evening that he believed she despised him, for she would never go in the street with him.

Defense: Did he never ask you to go in her presence?

Hope Sands: He once asked me to go to his brother's, but I could not conveniently; Elma was present. She said, "Why don't you ask me?" He replied, "I know you would not go if I did."

Defense: Did you not stop at some house on the way to church?

Hope Sands: Yes, we did; we stopped at Ezra Weeks's, the brother of Levi.

The cross-examination stopped at this point; obviously the defense felt that this was a good note on which to leave Hope Sands, who was a young lady who knew her

*A room set aside for Indian relics and a collection of curiosities in City Hall under the sponsorship of the Tammany Society.

own mind. The next witness for the prosecution was Elias Ring. Since he was a Quaker, he undoubtedly was dressed in a sombre coat and full trousers; his shoes would be wide and heavy. And he would not remove his low-crowned, wide-brimmed hat; Quaker men did not remove their hats in deference to any person or place. These hats had earned the men the nickname of "Broadbrims."

Elias Ring: Levi Weeks was a lodger in my house and in the ninth month—

Question by Defense: What month is that called?

Elias Ring: I don't know. Thee can tell.

Everyone knew, of course, that the ninth month was September. The defense were out to blacken Elias Ring's name, and the lawyer was speaking to him with some contempt, possibly only to rattle him. Elias, in his baggy clothes and wide hat, must have presented an interesting contrast to the defense attorneys: both Hamilton and Burr, at least, were small men, no taller than five feet six, but dapper, stylish and attractive to women. Hamilton was once described as wearing a blue coat with bright buttons and unusually long skirts, a white waistcoat, black silk small clothes and white silk stockings. Burr, who had strikingly deep hazel eyes, frequently wore a single-breasted blue jacket with a stand-up collar, a buff vest and dark trousers. His style at the bar was terser than Hamilton's. Brockholst Livingston was described as having "a fine Roman face; an aquiline nose, high forehead, bald head and projecting chin."[42]

Elias Ring: At this time, when my wife was gone into the country, Levi and Elma were constantly together in private. I was alone and very lonesome, and was induced to believe from their conduct that they were shortly to be married. Elma's bed was in the back room, on the second floor; the front room had a bed in it, in which Isaac Hatfield slept about three weeks. Hatfield during this time was occasionally out of town. I slept in the front room below; and one night when Hatfield was out of town, I heard a talking and noise in his room. In the morning I went up into the room and found the bed tumbled, and Elma's clothes which she wore in the afternoon, lying on the bed.

Mr Colden: Did you see her in the room?

Elias Ring: No; I saw nothing, but I have no doubt she was there, for Hatfield was not there then, and there was no other person in the house besides Levi and his apprentice, and Elma and myself.

Mr Colden: How late was it in the night, when you heard this noise?

Elias Ring: After twelve o'clock.

Question by one of the jury: Did Elma, do you suppose, get up from her bed, and go away naked?—You say she left her clothes.

Presumably, this remark was intended to raise some levity in the courtroom, not incidentally at Elias Ring's expense. It also undercut the importance of what he was saying, and subtly impugned Elma.

Elias Ring: She left part of her clothes. She had two

suits and this was part of the best, which she had on the day before, being first day.

Mr Colden: Did you see anything improper or immodest in the behavior of Elma, until she was acquainted with the prisoner?

This question may have been Mr Colden's rebuke to the amusement in the room at the suggestion that Elma was accustomed to appear in public unclothed.

Elias Ring: No, never.

With that, Mr Colden's examination ended, and the cross-examination began.

Defense: Did you ever see any intimacies between Levi Weeks and Margaret Clark?

Elias Ring: I have seen, formerly, some familiarities between them.

Defense: Did you never hear any noise when Hatfield slept in the room over you?

Elias Ring: No.

Defense: Did you ever know that the prisoner and Elma were in bed together?

Elias Ring: No.

Defense: What materials is the partition made of between Watkins' house and yours?

Elias Ring: It is a plank partition, lathed and plastered.

Defense: Could you hear the noise of children through?

Elias Ring: No; not as I can recollect.

Defense: Is Mr Watkins a clever man and a good neighbour?

Elias Ring: Yes, he is.

The defense were laying the groundwork for Mr Watkins to disparage Elias Ring's reputation. They could not have been pleased that Elias had never heard the noise of children's voices through the partition between the two houses, but the last question was intended to establish Mr Watkins' credibility out of Elias' own mouth. That subject was then quickly dropped.

Defense: Do you remember how Elma appeared on the twenty-second of December?

Elias Ring: She was as cheerful and gay, as ever I saw her.

Defense: Pray tell what you remember particularly about that day.

Elias Ring: On the twenty-second of December I had been to meeting in the afternoon; I returned and found Elma dressing, and my wife helping her in dressing and assisting her in putting on her gloves. About eight o'clock Elma went out, I saw her go out of the room, and I heard the front door open and shut about three or four minutes thereafter and my wife took the candle and went out and was gone about two minutes. The two boarders, Lacey and Russel, came in, and one of them pulled out his watch and observed it was eight o'clock.

Defense: What kind of gloves were they?

Elias Ring: Long white gloves.

Defense: Are you certain they were white?

Elias Ring: Yes, I saw my wife tie them on and took notice.

Defense: Did you hear her go upstairs?

This line of questioning—the two questions about the gloves, and the question about hearing "her" go upstairs—is somewhat baffling. The defense here was perhaps attempting to confuse the issue, to give the impression that Elias Ring was not a reliable witness in some way, or that they knew something about Elma's gloves which would later be significant. Certainly the question of the gloves did not come up again. And it is not clear to whom the defense was referring or to what point in the evening they were referring, when the counselor asked whether Mr Ring had heard "her" go upstairs. Elias Ring did not appear to understand the question.

Elias Ring: I am not certain that I heard anybody go upstairs. When my wife returned, I asked who went out? She said, "Elma and Levi." I answered that it was wrong, she would get sick. She replied, "He will be more careful of her than I would be."

About ten o'clock Levi came in. He asked if Hope had got home; my wife answered, "No."

He asked, "Is Elma gone to bed?"

She answered, "No, she is gone out."

He observed it was strange she should go out so late and alone.

Ring went on to corroborate his wife's testimony about the events of the rest of the evening.

Defense: Have you not threatened the prisoner at some time since this affair happened?

Elias Ring: I never threatened him that I know of—I had a conversation with him, in which he asked me if I had not said certain things about him, respecting Elma being missing, and he said if I told such things of him he would tell of me and Croucher.

Question by Mr Colden: Did you not tell him you believed him guilty?—How did he appear?

Elias Ring: I did, and he appeared as white as ashes, and trembled all over like a leaf.

The defense counsel resumed questioning.

Defense: What was the character of the prisoner previous to this, and how was he liked in the family?

Elias Ring: His character was always good, for anything I know, and his behaviour was such that he was generally esteemed.

Defense: Were you not the friend and protector of Elma?

Elias Ring: Yes.

Defense: Did you ever speak to her about her improper intimacy with Levi?

Elias Ring: I never did.

Defense: Did you hear any whispering in the entry or anybody come downstairs?

Elias Ring: I did not, for I set in the corner and was not attentive to these things.

Next were called the boarders and lodgers in the Ring boardinghouse, each in turn. First was Margaret Clark, nicknamed Peggy.

Margaret Clark: I lived at Mr Ring's about six months before Levi Weeks came to board there, and Gulielma Sands lived there. I went into the country on the twenty-eighth or twenty-ninth of August, on account of the fever, and returned about the twelfth of November.

Mr Colden: Did you not observe a very particular kind of attention in the prisoner, to Elma?

Margaret Clark: I can't say I did. I can't say I thought there was anything that looked like courting her.—After I returned, she and he appeared more intimate together, which I suppose arose from their having been together, and while I was in the country.

This testimony would seem to indicate that Miss Clark had been somewhat interested in Levi herself, and the implication seemed to be that because of her own absence Levi had turned to Elma as a second choice. It will be remembered that Catherine Ring had testified that when Levi had first come to board he had "showed attention" to Margaret Clark. Mr Colden, who apparently had not expected this sort of answer to his direct question, did not go into Margaret Clark's own attitude toward Levi and toward Elma, even though this witness was not very helpful to the prosecution case.

Mr Colden: Did you never know of their being locked up together?

Margaret Clark: I knew once of their being locked up together in the bedroom. Afterwards he told me they were in the bedroom together. This was the Monday evening before she was missing. Another time I saw him standing in her room when she was sick, but I thought nothing of this, because he was always attentive to anyone that was sick.

Mr Colden did not ask her who else in the house had been sick. But this question was to come up again in connection with the Watkins' testimony.

Mr Colden: Pray how long did you live in the house do you suppose?

Margaret Clark: I might have been absent half the time.

Question by Defense: Did not Levi pay as much attention to Hope Sands as he did to Elma?

Margaret Clark: Yes, I think he did, and more too.

She corroborated the testimony of other witnesses that Elma had had a cheerful temper.

The second boarder to testify was Isaac Hatfield, who had taken Elma's room while Catherine, her sister and her children were in Cornwall.

Isaac Hatfield: I lodged at Mr Ring's from the fourteenth or fifteenth of September, four or five weeks. I lodged in the front room on the second floor. I observed a great intimacy between the prisoner and the deceased, such as to induce me to suppose he was paying his addresses to her with a view to marry.

The next witness was the lodger, Richard David Croucher, a man of whom James Parton said "he had the mean, down look which is associated with the timidity of guilt."[43] He was suspected of having spread rumors about Levi's guilt and of having distributed handbills telling of ghosts and goblins appearing at the Manhattan Well.

R. D. Croucher: May it please the Court and the gentlemen of the jury, I was a lodger but not a boarder in Mr Ring's house. I remained at the house all the time of Mrs Ring's absence, and paid particular attention to the behaviour of the prisoner and the deceased, and I was satisfied from what I saw there was a warm courtship going on. I have known the prisoner at the bar to be with the deceased Elma Sands in private, frequently and all times of night. I knew him to pass two whole nights in her bedroom. Once lying in my bed, which stood in the middle of the room, and in a posture which was favorable to see who passed the door, and which I assumed on purpose—I had some curiosity—I saw the prisoner at the bar come out of her room, and pass the door in his shirt only, to his own room. Once too at a time when they were less cautious than usual, I saw them in *a very intimate* situation.

Mr Colden: Did you tell anyone of this?

R. D. Croucher: I never took notice of it to anyone.

As a witness Croucher was a little too forthcoming. His unpleasant appearance, combined with the common knowledge that he had worked hard to associate Levi Weeks with the murder, made him unconvincing. The defense saw him as a man who could himself be suspected of murder.

Defense: Pray what countryman are you?

R. D. Croucher: An Englishman. I have been in this country since January, 1799.

Defense: Where, sir, was you on the night of the twenty-second of December, 1799?

R. D. Croucher: I supped that night at Mrs Ashmore's, but that's not her real name—it is 884 Bowery lane—It was the birthday of her son—she has had a good deal of my money, and I thought I would go and sup with her.

I went accordingly. In the course of the evening when the deceased was missing, I crossed twice or three times from Greenwich-street to Broadway and was once at the coffee-house. I went out to the Bowery and returned to Mrs Ring's.

Defense: What time did you return home that night?

R. D. Croucher: It was my agreement with Mrs Ring

to be at home at ten o'clock a'nights but on this occasion I stayed out till eleven or half past eleven.

Defense: Do you know where the Manhattan Well is?

R. D. Croucher: I do.

Defense: Did you pass by it that evening?

R. D. Croucher: I did not—I wish I had—I might, perhaps, have saved the life of the deceased.

Defense: Have you not said you did?

R. D. Croucher: No. I might have said I wished I had.

Defense: Have you ever had a quarrel with the prisoner at the bar?

R. D. Croucher: I bear him no malice.

Defense: But have you never had any words with him?

R. D. Croucher: Once I had—the reason was this, if you wish me to tell it:—Going hastily upstairs, I suddenly came upon Elma, who stood at the door—she cried out Ah! and fainted away. On hearing this, the prisoner came down from his room and said it was not the first time I had insulted her. I told him he was an impertinent puppy. Afterwards, being sensible of his error, he begged my pardon.

Defense: And you say you bear him no ill will?

R. D. Croucher: I bear him no malice, but I despise every man who does not behave in character.

Defense: How near the Manhattan Well do you think you passed that night?

R. D. Croucher: I believe I might have passed the glue manufactory.

North of the city was a factory where glue was made from pigs' feet. Factories which gave off unpleasant fumes were required by law to be located outside the city limits.

Defense: Do you not know what route you took?

R. D. Croucher: I do not; I cannot certainly say, I might have passed by one route or another; I go sometimes by the road, sometimes across the field.

Defense: Was it dark?

R. D. Croucher: I believe there was little moonlight—the going was very bad.

Question by Mr Colden: Mr Croucher, have you ever heard any noise in the room of the prisoner at an uncommon time of night, since this affair happened?

R. D. Croucher: Yes, sir, I have. The night the deceased was missing and the next night, and every succeeding night while he stayed in the house, I heard him up whenever I waked at all times from eleven o'clock at night till four in the morning, and a continual noise, almost. I thought then his brother had some great work on hand and that he was drawing plans; but since I have accounted for it in a different way.

Defense: What kind of noises were these?

R. D. Croucher: The noise of moving about chairs, throwing down the tongs, and such kind of noises.

Defense: Were you ever upon any other than friendly terms with Elma?

R. D. Croucher: After I offended the prisoner at the bar, who she thought was an Adonis, I never spoke to her again.

The next prosecution witness, John Benson, had boarded at Mr Ring's during the yellow fever epidemic but, despite the fact that he had been called by Mr Colden, he said he did not see anything "very particular" in Levi's attentions to Elma. He said that Elma was "a girl of a lively, cheerful disposition;" this opinion was echoed by Henry Reynolds who had known Elma since she was a child. They had grown up together.

Levi Weeks's apprentice, William Anderson, was called. Apprentices were boys "bound out" or placed under contract to work in return for board and training for a specified number of years. Apprentice contracts were made before a magistrate, according to Benjamin Franklin, and obliged the master to provide his charge with "meat, drink, apparel, washing and lodging" and, when the contract ended, to supply him "with a compleat new suit of clothes." The apprentice was to be taught to read and write and "cast accompts."[44] After the apprenticeship was ended, if the boy wished to ply his master's trade he was usually restricted from doing it within a specified distance of the master's shop.

William Anderson: I never saw anything to make me suppose that my master was more particular in his attentions to Elma than to the other two, Margaret and Hope. One day my master said to me, "You must not think it strange of my keeping Elma's company—it is not for courtship nor dishonor, but only for conversation."

One night I pretended to be asleep, and the prisoner undressed himself, and came with the candle and looked to see if I was asleep or not. Supposing I was, he went downstairs in his shirt, and did not come back until morning.

Mr Colden: Did your master always sleep with you?

William Anderson: Yes.

Mr Colden: How did he rest the night Elma was missing, and the next?

William Anderson: He slept as well as usual the night Elma was missing, and Monday and Tuesday nights, but on Wednesday night, near day, he sighed out in his sleep, "Oh! Elmore!"

He agreed with the other witnesses that Elma was of a lively, cheerful disposition, but he thought she appeared less so that day before she was missing—probably Sunday, the twenty-second.

Colden's calling of the next witness was a tactical error that cost him dearly. Susanna Broad, described by Coleman as "an aged and very infirm woman," was so obviously confused that her testimony overshadowed, in the minds of those predisposed toward the defense, the strong case presented by previous prosecution witnesses.

Susanna Broad: I live opposite Ezra Weeks's lumberyard, and on the night when the deceased was lost,

> I heard the gate open and a sleigh or carriage come out of the yard about eight o'clock. It made a rumbling noise, but had no bells on it, and that it was not gone long before it returned again.

Mr Colden asked no questions, and the defense began cross-examination.

Defense: How did you know it was eight o'clock?

Susanna Broad: Because my son and daughter was gone to meeting and meeting is done about eight o'clock.

Defense: Had your son and daughter returned before the sleigh went out?

Susanna Broad: I don't know what they had, I believe they had not then.

Defense: Had they returned before the sleigh came back?

Susanna Broad: They were abed.

Defense: When was this, what month was it?

Susanna Broad: I don't know the month, I know it was so.

Defense: Was it after Christmas, or before Christmas?

Susanna Broad: It was after, I believe; it was in January.

Defense: That you are sure of, it was in January you say?

Susanna Broad: Yes; I am sure it was in January.

Defense: Did you ever hear this gate open before?

Susanna Broad: No gentlemen; do you think I came here to tell a lie?

Defense: Nor since?

Susanna Broad: No, gentlemen, no.

Defense: When did you first remember about this sleigh being taken out?

Susanna Broad: When I saw this young woman at Mrs Ring's and helped to lay her out.

Question by Mr Colden: Did you observe any marks of violence when you laid her out?

Susanna Broad: I found no bruises except on the right shoulder where I felt and it was soft, but I thought her neck was broke.

Mr Colden's next witnesses were people who had been abroad or had tales to tell of the night of December twenty-second. It should perhaps be pointed out here that the streets of New York in 1799 were very dark at night. Thirty-eight years earlier, with much fanfare and excitement, whale-oil lamps had been placed on poles in the streets. But these proved to be a disappointment: the light they shed was dim at best and they were not properly maintained. Soot accumulated on the glass, wicks went untrimmed and if a light went out it was not lit again. On Nassau Street, only a few yards from the mayor's house, a man was severely injured when he walked into a pump; there was not a single lighted lamp in the area. In addition to insufficient light and poor maintenance, on those several nights each month when bright moonlight was expected, the lights were not lit at all. A committee was appointed to improve the situation, and in 1798 the nights in the month on which lamps must be lit were increased from twenty-one to twenty-four, but this was not much help.[45]

Catherine Lyon had been abroad that Sunday night.

Catherine Lyon: On the Sunday night before Christmas, being in Greenwich street at the pump near the door of the new Furnace, I saw Gulielma, a little after eight o'clock. Myself was attending a lame woman who lay in the street, and Elma came up to me alone, and asked who it was. There was a good many people passing, and I could not say if they was with her or not; but I heard somebody say, *"Let's go"* and the deceased bid me good night and went on. There was men passing before and behind, but whether in company with her I could not tell. About a half an hour or less after I saw Elma, I heard from the fields behind the hill at Lispenards a cry in a woman's voice of *"Murder, murder!* Oh, save me!"

The defense began cross-examination.

Defense: Did you see the face of Elma?

Catherine Lyon: I did not, but I knew her form and shape.

Defense: Did you see any sleigh at this time, when you saw the girl?

Catherine Lyon: No, I did not.

Defense: Where were you when you heard the cry you speak of?

Catherine Lyon: In the front of Lispenards.

Defense: How long after you saw this woman you suppose to be Elma?

Catherine Lyon: About half an hour.

The defense would of course find the alleged cry for help in conflict with their position that Elma had committed suicide.

It was also necessary that they attempt to discredit the testimony of Margaret Freeman, another pedestrian on that Sunday night, who claimed to have seen a sleigh. If Elma were riding in a sleigh, she was not alone, and she could not have rushed, distraught, from the Ring house to fling herself into the Manhattan Well.

Margaret Freeman: On the Sunday night before Christmas, in the upper part of Greenwich street, as I and my children was coming home from meeting, I was holding my boy by the arm, a one-horse sleigh overtook me as I was walking in the middle of the road, with two men and a woman in it, all talking and laughing very lively, particularly the woman; I kept out of the way for it to pass. When I came in I ran upstairs, and looking at the watch, I saw it was a quarter past eight. The watch was rather slow.

She was immediately cross-examined.

Defense: How long ago is it since you were first applied to, respecting this affair?

Margaret Freeman: Four or five weeks ago—Three or four weeks after the sleigh overtook me.

Defense: Are you sure, Mrs Freeman, that this was before Christmas?

Margaret Freeman: I am positive it was.

Defense: What meeting was it you had been to?

Margaret Freeman: The Methodist church.

Defense: Did you ever see Ezra Weeks's sleigh anywhere?

Margaret Freeman: I don't know as I ever did.

Defense: Was it a dark night?

Margaret Freeman: Not very dark, but the moon did not shine.

The sleigh, which the defense found very troublesome, came up again in the testimony of William Lewis.

William Lewis: On the Monday morning before Christmas, I and my wife was coming to town in a wood sleigh, and I discovered the track of a one-horse sleigh about three hundred feet from the Manhattan Well, up the new road which Colonel Burr had built, and I found the sleigh had drove so near the wall, that I observed it was a wonder it had not turned over. I had passed that way the Sunday morning before, and there was no track there then; the sleigh appeared to have gone up toward the Balloon house. I thought somebody had missed their way, for there was no road there, and this made me so particular in my observation. I observed that there was one board off the Well, which left it open, it may be twelve or thirteen inches—there was tracks of people round the Well.

On cross-examination the defense attempted to discredit even the possibility that a sleigh had been seen anywhere near the Manhattan Well on that Sunday night.

Defense: Is not that road a very bad one?

William Lewis: Yes.

Defense: Is it not so bad that nobody could drive there in the night, even slowly, without great danger?

William Lewis: The road is bad, but I think I would have gone it.

Defense: Do you think you could have found the Well in the night?

William Lewis: I could have found it in the darkest night that ever was; it would only be to keep along close by the fence.

Mr Lewis was a positive man who refused to be shaken. His wife, Ann Lewis, corroborated his testimony.

But other people said they had seen the sleigh. The next witnesses were Buthrong Anderson and two of his friends, Joseph Stringham and Joseph Cornwell.

Buthrong Anderson: I was sent for by a neighbour to go to a christening. I had been to Mr Pilmore's church—I live in William street, No. 128. It was the Sunday before Christmas; I went out of meeting with company, up the Bowery, as far as the two-mile stone, and down Broadway.

The two-mile stone marked the distance from what was then the center of the city. Broadway, a wide, handsome street at the Battery, narrowed down to a country lane before it ended. It would have been difficult for two vehicles to pass abreast in that lane.

Buthrong Anderson: On my return down the middle-road, I was overtaken by a one-horse sleigh about half-past eight in the evening—on a full gallop, with two or three men or women in it; I can't say whether they were men or women. The horse seemed to be dark-colored.

Mr Colden: Have you not, sir, seen Ezra Weeks drive a horse that appeared to you of the same size and color with this?

Buthrong Anderson: I have seen him drive such a one, I think.

Cross-examination began.

Defense: Do you pretend to distinguish the color of a horse in the night?

Buthrong Anderson: Not exactly—but I know he was not light-colored.

Defense: Can you determine the size of a horse when he is on a gallop, and as you say, on a full gallop?

Buthrong Anderson: I think he was such a sized horse as I have described him.

Joseph Stringham and Joseph Cornwell were in the sleigh with Anderson, and corroborated his testimony. Coleman says, "They fixed the Sunday to be after Thanksgiving, which was the nineteenth December." Thanksgiving was not yet a national holiday, but was celebrated at the discretion of local authorities. On Monday, December 16, 1799, the Common Council of the City of New York proclaimed "Thursday next"—which would be December 19—as Thanksgiving Day.

Stringham and Cornwell added that when the single sleigh passed them at full gallop they "huzzaed, as is usual on such occasions" but the riders took no notice of them.

Two witnesses followed, a husband and wife, Lawrence and Arnetta Van Norden.

Arnetta Van Norden: We live about half-way from Broadway to the Well. About eight or nine o'clock in the evening, my husband heard a noise, and he stood up and observed it was from the Well. I then looked through the window, and we heard a woman cry out from towards the Well, "Lord have mercy on me, Lord help me."

Lawrence Van Norden: On the Sunday that the girl was missing, I found by calculation after she was found in the Well, it was the same—I heard the voice of a woman cry out, "Oh, Lord have mercy upon me! What shall I do? Help me!" I got up and looked out of the window; it was a clear night, starlight. I got up out of bed to hear and see what I could, and I looked out of the window towards the Well. I can see the Well from my house, and I heard this noise that I tell you of, and I looked then to the Well, and I saw a man walking near the Well, about the Well. In a little time the cries stopped and I went to bed again.

This rather strange report elicited a dry and business-like cross-examination of Lawrence Van Norden.

Defense: How near do you live to this Well?

Lawrence Van Norden: About a hundred yards.

Defense: Was there snow on the ground?

Lawrence Van Norden: Yes.

Defense: Did you see a sleigh at the same time?

Lawrence Van Norden: No.

Since this reply painfully demolished points made for the prosecution by preceding witnesses, Mr Colden was stirred to interject a question.

Question by Mr Colden: Might there not have been a sleigh there which you could not see from your chamber window? I'll put the question a little more particularly—Is not the make of the ground such, that if a sleigh was standing near the fence at the Well, you would look over it from your window, in looking at the Well?

Lawrence Van Norden: I don't know, I never minded.

Defense: Is there any house near yours?

Lawrence Van Norden: There is one, a red house about [sic] yards off.

Defense: Did you go to the Well the next morning to make any examination?

Lawrence Van Norden: No.

Defense: Did you mention this, or what you saw and heard to anybody the next day?

Lawrence Van Norden: Not as I can remember.

At this point the Assistant Attorney General went from one fiasco to another. He called two young boys, Thomas Gray, eleven years old, and Samuel Smith, thirteen. They had been with a third boy, William Blanck, when he fished Elma's muff out of the Well. These boys were asked if they knew what an oath was. They replied that they did not. They were asked if they could read, and said that they could not. They said also that they did not know what an oath required of them. Consequently they were rejected as incompetent witnesses. This did not reflect well on Mr Colden, nor did the response of a third witness, Jacob Campbell, who testified that he knew nothing "about this affair of my own knowledge."

The Assistant Attorney General had better luck with Henry Orr, who was at least an admissible witness with a statement to make.

Henry Orr: On the twenty-second of December, after dark, I went from my house near the Union Furnace, to a house near Mr Benson's, and I stayed there, I should judge, about an hour, and then came down, and when I got near Lewis' fence, I heard a cry in the direction of the Baloon house. It was the voice of a woman, towards the Well, in distress. When I got nearer the Well I heard another cry, but the second cry was not so loud as the first, but rather smothered.

This was Mr Orr's entire statement, and the defense did not spend much time on cross-examining him.

Defense: When was this—what time in the evening?

Henry Orr: It was six or seven minutes before, or six or seven minutes after nine.

Defense: How did you know that this was the time?

Henry Orr: I am sure it was near nine when I left Henry Luther's, the cartman, near Colonel Benson's.

These short visits—ranging from twenty minutes to, in this case, "about an hour"—were commonplace social calls of the time. With little available public entertainment, the evening was thus whiled away.

Mr Colden called William Blanck, the boy who had fished Elma's muff from the Well. The Court asked him his age, and he responded that he was "about thirteen." He acknowledged that he could not read although he had been at school; but he sometimes said his prayers. Like the other two boys, he did not know what an oath was, and like them he was set aside as incompetent.

A practical plan for tax-supported education in the young Republic had not yet evolved; for the most part the education of children from families who could or would not pay for expensive tutoring was left to the churches.

Mr Colden, once more embarrassed, called the boy's father, Andrew Blanck.

Mr Colden: Pray sir, what is your son's age?

Andrew Blanck: He is thirteen.

Question by the Court: Can he read?

Andrew Blanck: No, I believe he cannot.

The Court: Go on, sir.

Andrew Blanck: One day my son brought home a muff which he said he got in the Well. I went the next day to the Well and looked in, but I saw nothing. I discovered a sleigh track about eight or ten feet from the Well, and I saw men's tracks to the Well and about it, and a good deal of tracking on the lower side of it; one man's track I noticed from the Well to the road.

Mr Colden: Will you describe the track—was it large or small?

Andrew Blanck: The foot was large, with a heel to it, flat.

At that time shoes were not designed to differentiate between right and left feet; the design was to be introduced within the year.

Catherine Ring was called back and asked what kind of shoes Elma wore. She said that Elma's shoes had no heels, and that her feet were slim and rather long. Mr Blanck was recalled and cross-examined.

Defense: What day was this, sir?

Andrew Blanck: The muff was found the day before Christmas, and I went there on Christmas day.

Question by Mr Colden: What sort of sleigh track was it you saw?

Andrew Blanck: A one-horse sleigh.

It was now one-thirty in the morning. Court had been in session continuously for fifteen hours and the prosecution had not yet finished presenting its case. The jurors requested an adjournment until the next day, because it appeared likely that the trial would last until the following night. The Court was reluctant to adjourn, but some members of the jury said that they were falling asleep and could not concentrate on the testimony. The Court then decided to adjourn until ten o'clock the next day. The constables were sworn to keep the jury together until morning "in some private and convenient place; and two more were sent to wait upon them and bring them what refreshments they might want."

Adjournments of this kind were unusual; most trials lasted only a single day. And where in the city could the jurors be sequestered in the middle of the night? It was finally decided that they could sleep in the "picture room" in the City Hall, so called because portraits hung there of the King and Queen of France, Columbus, Washington and several Revolutionary War heroes.

CHAPTER FIVE

PROSECUTION CONTINUED

The trial resumed on Tuesday, April 1, at ten o'clock in the morning. The prosecution called Dr Richard C. Skinner.

Mr Colden: Doctor Skinner, are you not a surgeon in this city, and did not you see the body of Elma Sands after it was taken out of the Well, and examine it? Pray, sir, inform the court and jury.

Dr Skinner: I follow a branch of surgery, but I do not pretend to be a professed surgeon. I am a dentist, but I have made the subject of surgery generally my study. I saw the corpse of the deceased twice. I had but a superficial view, however, of it as it lay in the coffin, exposed to the view of thousands. I examined such parts as were come-at-able—Such as her head, neck and breast. I discovered several bruises and scratches, particularly a bruise upon the forehead and chin, and upon the left breast or near it.

Question by the Court: How long was this after she was taken out of the water?

Dr Skinner: I do not know.

Mr Colden: Will you describe those marks more particularly?

Dr Skinner: I think that the mark upon the neck had the appearance of a compression, but not by a rope or handkerchief. It was suggested by a number that the neck was broken and I examined it and discovered that it was not.

Question by the Court: What was the color of the spots?

Dr Skinner: Those on the neck were reddish black spots. There were several small spots which might have passed unnoticed by a common observer. The appearance upon the breast was about as large as the circumference of a dollar; it was a small bruise, but it was more difficult to examine than the other: there was a number of women present.

Mr Colden(?) The Court(?): Was the compression which you spoke of round her neck, such as might have been made by the hand?

Dr Skinner: My impression then was and now is that it was.

Mr Colden(?) The Court(?): As to the scratches of which you speak?

Dr Skinner: They were small such as might arise from a nail.

Mr Colden: Well sir, go on and describe what you saw.

Dr Skinner: On the forehead and chin, the contusion was not very large, but the skin was broken.

Mr Colden: Were you acquainted with Mr and Mrs Ring?

Dr Skinner: I did not know any of the parties.

Question by the Court: Doctor Skinner, was the appearance such as might have been produced by the frost?

Dr Skinner: I do not think it was.

Question by the Court: Would not the immersion in the water, or frost give the appearance that you mention, of those livid spots?

Dr Skinner: I think not, but am not certain.

Mr Colden: Were the spots in a chain round the neck?

Dr Skinner: There were several spots pretty much in a row on the neck.

Mr Colden turned the witness over to the defense for cross-examination. The prosecution was later to be criticized for bringing to the stand a dentist with an interest in surgery rather than a qualified doctor and one who had had an opportunity to examine the body thoroughly. In addition to his apparent lack of credentials, Dr Skinner appeared under questioning to be somewhat uncertain and possibly intimidated by the defense attorneys, as well as by the judges.

Defense: Do you say, sir, you are certain that the spots were in a ring round the neck?

Dr Skinner: I cannot say that they were in an exact circle, not particularly; I think they were regular, but cannot exactly say.

Defense: Were they, sir, spots or lines?

Dr Skinner: They were small spots, not lines.

Defense: May such spots not have happened from a different mode than that of strangulation?

Dr Skinner: I am incapable of judging how they might have happened.

Question by Mr Colden: Suppose, Doctor, a person had been strangled by hand, would it not have left such an appearance upon the body?

Dr Skinner: I think it would.

Mr Colden's next witness was James W. Lent, one of the men who had brought Elma's body out of the Well.

James Lent: On the second of January last, I together with Mr Page, had some business to do in breaking a horse, and we went up to Andrew Blanck's and we dined there: Blanck insisted upon it. While we were dining, two persons, Mr Watkins and Mr Elias Ring, came there to get hooks and poles to sound the Manhattan Well for the body of a young woman who was supposed to be drowned. We got the poles and went all together to the Well, which we uncovered.

Page took the pole first and said he thought he felt her; I took hold then and thought I felt her too. Watkins drove in the nails, I took the pole and hooked the nail in her clothes and drew her up carefully to the top of the water. As soon as Mr Ring saw her calico gown he said it was she, he knew the gown. She was so heavy now we could not draw her out by the nail and the little boy went for a rope to the next house, while I held her still.

I put the rope under her and drew her up gently; she slewed round but there was not a thread of her clothes which touched either side of the Well. When she was drawn up we laid her on a plank, and she appeared in such a situation as if she had been murdered.

Interjection by Defense: You are to tell what you saw, not what conclusion you made. That is for the jury.

The Court: Proceed.

James Lent: Her hat was off, her gown torn open just above the waist, her shawl was off and her handkerchief and shoes was gone; her hair hung over her head. In lifting her up, I found her head fell forward and when we lifted her a little back her head fell back again, and again it fell to the right, which caused me to suppose her neck was broke. She had a white dimity petticoat on. I discovered on her right hand something like a kick, there was the scratches of sand upon her skin, some of which was knocked off and seemed to have been drove forward. Her stockings were torn at the toes; the right foot was bare and somewhat scratched; the scratches were on the upper part of the foot, as if she had been dragged on the ground.

Question by the Court: Did you examine her body?

James Lent: I did not—the stockings, as far as could be seen without lifting up the petticoat, was whole and good.

The Court(?): Were there any bruises upon the face?

James Lent: I do not recollect—there might have been.

The Court: Might you not have injured the head with the pole?

James Lent: Not at all—the pole did not touch her head; I was particularly tender with it—I hooked her in the skirt of her gown.

The Court(?): Were her limbs stiff?

James Lent: Her arms were—her legs were straight, but her neck was remarkably limber.

The Court(?): How did her countenance appear?

James Lent: It looked like a person who had been walking against the wind—flush but not so much so as she appeared a few days after. Her appearance was horrid enough—her hat and cap off, her hair hanging all over her head, her comb was yet hanging in her hair, tied with a white ribbon; her shawl was off; her gown was torn open with great violence, and her shoes were off.

The Court(?): Was the string of her gown broke or the collar torn?

James Lent: I did not discover that they were—It appeared as if the knot by which they had been tied, had slipped.

Question by one of the jury: Were the fingers bruised?

James Lent: They seemed jambed, like a kick.

One of the jury(?): Did you see sand, and what kind of sand?

James Lent: I did not see any sand, but the marks of sand, as it seemed.

Question by Defense: How do you know the scratches were made up or down?

James Lent: It only appeared so to me.

I went to the police, and then with the officer to find the prisoner; we stayed a little back till we saw the officer tap him on the shoulder. I then went up to him, he stood in the door.

I says, "Is this the young man?"

He replies, "Yes."

I told him I was very sorry for his situation—I felt affected—I expressed it to him—

He turned about and said, "It is too hard," and he dropped his head and said, "Is it the Manhattan Well she was found in?"

I said I knew not what Well she was found in—I did not then know the Manhattan Well—this was about half past three in the afternoon; however, I don't know exactly the time but by calculation. I suppose the body was found about fifteen minutes after we had left Blanck's house.

Question by one of the jury: Was there any mention made of the Manhattan Well in the presence of the prisoner before he asked the question?

James Lent: I did not hear any, I don't believe there was.

One of the jury(?): Was you present when he first saw the body—what did he say?

The defense objected, saying that this was an improper question, but was overruled by the Court. This was the first time the Court had ruled against the defense.

James Lent: In proceeding to the Well, he asked for his brother as counsel for him—when we came there we found a great number of people collected—I stepped before him and said, "Weeks, do you know that young woman that lies there a corpse?"

He said, "I think I know the gown."

"My young friend," said I, "that is not the question I ask you. Is there no marks in that countenance you know?"

He turned himself and said, "I think there is."

Mr Colden(?): Was she not a natural corpse?

James Lent: It seemed so—she looked as if she was asleep, seemingly—I never saw her alive.

Question by one of the jury: How long after he was taken before he asked if she was found in the Manhattan Well?

James Lent: I don't exactly know how many minutes.

It is interesting to note that the defense did not cross-examine James Lent. He was a convincing, lively, articulate and perceptive witness, and his testimony was damaging to the defense case. Obviously he could not be shaken or intimidated, and the best course for them was to get him off the stand as quickly as possible, and hope the jury would forget him.

The prosecution called a second physician, Dr James Snedecher.

Mr Colden: Pray sir, are you not a physician and live in this city?

Dr Snedecher: I am a physician and live in Barley street, twenty-eight years of age. I saw the body the second or third day after it was taken out of the Well. I was informed that it was much injured, and I examined it. There was many discolorations on the teguments of the skin. There was a dislocation of the clavicle from the sternum.

Mr Colden: Be so good, sir, as to speak in less technical language so that the jury may understand you.

Dr Snedecher: I thought the left collar bone was broke. Her fingers appeared to have been scratched from the knuckles down; there were many dislocations. I saw a mark upon her breast as large as a dollar, black and blue. Hearing that her neck was injured, I examined it, but I did not find it so.

The defense came forward for cross-examination.

Defense: Do you say the bone was broke, sir?

Dr Snedecher: The dislocations induced me to think the bone was broke and I run my thumbs one over another and I thought I felt that the bones were dislocated from the breastbone.

Question by the Court: Is it not common for a body to assume such an appearance as this had, in the first stage of putrefaction where there had been no violence committed on it?

Dr Snedecher: I do not think it is.

Defense: Will cold or immersion in water, or sudden suffocation, produce such an appearance?

Dr Snedecher: I don't pretend to say whether it will or no.

Defense: Does not a corpse exposed to the air put on a livid appearance?

Dr Snedecher: Yes, it does.

Mr Colden's third medical witness was David Hosack, who was personal physician to the city's elite, including

Burr and Hamilton—Dr Hosack was to attend Hamilton after he was shot by Burr in 1804. Dr Hosack's name appeared on the roster of every philanthropic, scientific, patriotic and educational organization in New York. He had graduated from Princeton in 1789, and had studied medicine under Samuel Bard and medicine and botany at the University of Edinburgh. He is remembered now as a botanist, since in 1801 he was to found the Elgin Botantical Gardens, a tract of about twenty acres on which Rockefeller Center stands, and where he grew a famous collection of medicinal plants and cultivated specimens of foreign and American trees and shrubs. He had instituted with some success the sudorific method of treating yellow fever—a treatment which, if it did nothing else, kept the patient from being bled or heavily dosed with mercury. He was one of the first American doctors to recognize the value of the stethoscope and to recommend vaccination against smallpox. He was considered to be a remarkably able diagnostician; when he was asked to explain his success, he said it was important to pay heed to first impressions which he believed were likely to be accurate since they were freer of bias. Among his other accomplishments, he was one of the founders of Bellevue Hospital.

Mr Colden: Did you see the body, sir, and when and what was its appearance?

Dr Hosack: I do not recollect the exact day, but curiosity led me in common with many others to visit the body; it lay exposed in a coffin. I remember it was upon the same day the body was interred.

Mr Colden: How long was this, sir, after it was taken out of the water?—Pray inform us what you saw?

Dr Hosack: The only appearance which attracted my particular attention was an unusual redness of the countenance; and upon looking at the neck, I observed three or four dark-colored spots, of an irregular shape, but not in an exact line as if they had been produced by a cord, but rather the effect of a violent pressure upon the neck—the hands were exposed, and I observed upon the backs of them several scratches.

Mr Colden: Did you examine the collar bone?

Dr Hosack: I did not.

Mr Colden: Could such appearances as you saw have been produced by suffocation merely?

Dr Hosack: I ascribed the unusual redness of the countenance to the sudden extinction of life, and the exposure to air. For in the many cases of sudden death by opium, lightning, poison, or a blow on the head, the florid appearance of the countenance has that appearance.

Mr Colden: Are you not, sir, decidedly of opinion that the livid spots which you have described, were the effect of violence?

Dr Hosack: I am.

Mr Colden: Could any person, in your opinion, have committed such an act of violence on their own person to have produced such effects?

Dr Hosack: I do not think it could be done.

Question by the Court: Could such a change have been produced by immersion in water?

Dr Hosack: I do not think it could.

The Court(?): Suppose there had been this immersion, would it have required to be exposed any length of time in the air to produce the spots?

Dr Hosack: The appearance some distance of time after death will be different from what it is immediately.

Question by Defense: Would the hand, by grasping the neck violently, produce such effects as you mention?

Dr Hosack: I believe it would.

Defense(?): What was the bigness of the spots round the neck?

Dr Hosack: The largest spots, those near the windpipe, were about an inch and a half, the smallest might be three quarters of an inch. I still think that the livid spots which I saw were the effect of injury done.

The defense did not cross-examine Dr Hosack. He could only damage their case for suicide, such as it was. They had other medical witnesses of their own to come. The prosecution called Elizabeth Osborn.

Elizabeth Osborn: I had a slight acquaintance with Elma Sands. On the twenty-second of December, I lent her my muff, she came to borrow it herself, and I observed that she was very neatly dressed, and she seemed to be very lively and very happy.

Mr Colden: When was the muff brought home to you?

Elizabeth Osborn: It was brought home the day she was found, and it appeared as if it had been wet.

Mr Colden: Did you understand it was found in the Well?

Elizabeth Osborn: I did.

Here there was an evident interjection by the defense with, Coleman says, "some conversation arising, as to the time the muff was found, it was admitted by the Attorney-General, that it was found some days before the body was discovered."

This witness was dismissed without cross-examination. Her contribution to the prosecution's enlightenment of the jury appears confined to her statement that Elma had been lively and very happy on the last Sunday of her life. The Attorney General's "admission" that the muff was found some days before the body was discovered offered a possible explanation for Levi's question to James Lent about the body being found in the Manhattan Well.

The prosecution's last witnesses were three men who testified about the possibility of Ezra Weeks's horse having been used to take Elma to the Well. "Mr Williams," Coleman writes, "testified that at the request of the Attorney-General, he had made an experiment in what time a man might drive a horse the most usual rout [sic] from Ring's to the Manhattan Well, and from there back again to Ezra Week's [sic] down Barley-street, and that although the roads were bad, he performed it once in 15 minutes and once in 16, without going out of a trot."

Sylvester Buskirk corroborated Mr Williams' testimony, and added that Ezra Weeks's horse had stood in his stable for sale, and Mr Buskirk apparently having examined it then, he declared that it looked like a good horse. The last witness, Mr Cross, said that he knew the Weeks horse, that it was indeed a good horse, and he thought it could go a mile in five minutes.

Here the prosecution closed its case, with Mr Colden reading a passage from *Essays: The Laws of Evidence by John Morgan* (1789) pleading for the acceptance of circumstantial evidence:

> Circumstantial evidence is all that can be expected, and indeed all that is necessary to substantiate such a charge. The prejudice entertained against receiving circumstantial evidence is carried to a pitch wholly inexcusable. In such a case as this it must be received, because the nature of the enquiry, for the most part, does not admit of any other; and, consequently, it is the best evidence that can possibly be given. But taking it in a more general sense, a concurrence of circumstances (which we must always suppose to be properly authenticated, otherwise they weigh nothing) forms a stronger ground of belief than positive and direct testimony affords, especially when unconfirmed by circumstances. The reason of this is obvious: a positive allegation may be founded in mistake, or, what is too common, in the perjury of the witness; but circumstances cannot lie; and a long chain of well connected fabricated circumstances, requires

an ingenuity and skill rarely to be met with; and such a consistency in the persons who come to support those circumstances by their oaths, as the annals of our courts of justice can seldom produce. Besides, circumstantial evidence is much more easily discussed, and much more easily contradicted by testimony if false, than the positive and direct allegation of a fact, which, being confined to the knowledge of an individual, cannot possibly be the subject of contradiction founded merely on presumption and probability.

CHAPTER SIX

CASE FOR THE DEFENSE

The defense opened its case: Aaron Burr gave the address to the jury. This is one of the few examples of Burr's style at the bar to be preserved:

> *Gentlemen of the Jury,*
>
> The patience with which you have listened to this lengthy and tedious detail of testimony is honorable to your characters. It evinces your solicitude to discharge the awful duties which are imposed upon you, and it affords a happy presage, that your minds are not infected by that blind and indiscriminating prejudice which had already marked the prisoner for its victim.
>
> You have relieved me from my greatest anxiety, for I know the unexampled industry that has been exerted to destroy the reputation of the accused, and to immolate him at the shrine of persecution without the solemnity of a candid and impartial trial. I know that hatred, revenge and cruelty, all the vindictive and ferocious passions have assembled in terrible array and exerted every engine to gratify their malice. The thousand tongues of rumour have been steadily employed in the fabrication and

dissemination of falsehoods, and every method has been taken to render their slanders universal. We have witnessed the extraordinary means which have been adopted to enflame the public passions and to direct the fury of popular resentment against the prisoner. Why has the body been exposed for days in the public streets in a manner the most indecent and shocking?—to attract the curiosity and arouse the feelings of numberless spectators. Such dreadful scenes speak powerfully to the passions: they petrify the mind with horror—congeal the blood within our veins—and excite the human bosom with irresistible, but undefineable emotions. When such emotions are once created they are not easily subdued.

It has happened in this case, that there have been attempts made to call up public sensibility, to excite resentment against this unfortunate man; in this way, gentlemen, the public opinion comes to be formed unfavourably, and long before the prisoner is brought to his trial he is already condemned. It is not to be supposed that these rumours can have any weight with a Court of Justice, but no man is altogether above being moved by such reports—and it requires some fortitude to withstand them; but now having heard the whole which can be said, you are prepared to determine whether the witnesses have always spoken with candor, or whether they have not spoken from temper, hatred and revenge.

We rely on it at first that there is nothing from which a discreet Jury can condemn the prisoner; in the very commencement of the business it is involved in doubt. Notwithstanding there may be testimony of an intimacy having subsisted between the prisoner and the deceased, we shall show you that there was nothing like a real courtship, or such a course of conduct as ought to induce impartial people to entertain a belief that marriage was intended; for it will be seen that she manifested equal partiality for other persons as for Mr Weeks. It will be shewn that she was in the habit of being frequently out of evenings, and could give no good account of herself; that she had at some time asserted that she had past the evening at houses, where it afterwards appeared she had not been. We shall show you that if suspicions may attach any where, there are those on whom they may be fastened with more appearance of truth than on the prisoner at the bar. Certainly you are not in this place to condemn others, yet it will relieve your minds of a burden. There will be two modes of giving a solution—first, that the deceased sometimes appeared melancholy, that she was a dependant upon this family, and that a gloomy sense of her situation might have led her to destroy herself. As to the incident of the sleigh, we shall account for his whole time during that evening, except about 15 minutes, which was employed in walking from one house to another; and we shall show you, that the whole of his conduct has been such, as totally to repel the idea of guilt. It will appear, that at ten o'clock the same evening, he supped at his brother's perfectly tranquil. The story you will see, is broken, disconnected, and utterly impossible.—We shall show you that the sleigh of Ezra Weeks was not out that evening, indeed the testimony of the good old woman was such, as could not gain the least belief, especially when you see that in matter of date and time she was totally lost: It will be shown you that on this occasion there have been violent attempts to inflame the public mind against the prisoner, and if we shall bring these home to some of the witnesses, we hope you will pronounce them altogether unworthy of credit—for a man to forestall the public opinion, is to arrest the hand of justice and deserves the severest reprehension, and such conduct we shall fix on the witnesses.

We shall show you that the prisoner has been uniformly well spoken of, more highly esteemed than one of his years, not only for his deportment, but for his morals. That a man of such a character should be impelled, without motive, to the commission of so horrid a crime, cannot be believed. Much has been said about the appearance of guilt and terror in the prisoner when charged with the crime. But, gentlemen, no man is armed with so much firmness of nerves that when charged with a crime, he will not discover great emotion; when, therefore, persons of little discernment come forward and say that they saw emotions of alarm and terror, no man however innocent as an angel, is safe; the emotions of surprize may be construed by the ignorant or the malicious into those of guilt. A man charged with a henious crime may even prevaricate; we shall show you the case of a young man, who, being charged with the crime of murder, even brought a young woman dressed to resemble the one he was charged with murdering—this was supposed to be a circumstance so conclusive of his guilt that he was convicted and executed, and afterwards the young woman was found to be alive. Even in this very city a case had occurred, not many years ago, a young man had been charged with the crime of rape. It is yet fresh in the minds of every body. The public mind was there highly incensed, and even after the unfortunate man had been acquitted by a verdict of a jury, so irritated and enflamed were the people, that the magistrates were insulted, and they threatened to pull down the house of the prisoner's counsel. After that a civil suit was commenced for the injury done the girl, a very enormous sum given in damages, and the defendant was ignominiously confined within the walls of a prison. Now it has come out that the accusation was certainly false and malicious.

If this doctrine of presumptive evidence is to prevail, and to be sufficient to convict, what remorse of conscience must a juror feel for having convicted a man who afterwards appeared to be innocent. In cases depending upon a chain of circumstance, all the fabric must hang together or the whole will tumble down. We shall, however, not depend altogether on the weakness of proof on the part of the prosecution, we shall bring forward such proof as will not leave to you even to balance in your

> minds, whether the prisoner is Guilty or Not—from even that burden we shall relieve you.
>
> But before we come to the testimony, on the part of the prisoner, it may be well to examine a little more into the nature of the evidence on the part of the prosecution. It may be material to discover how much of this testimony which we have heard is the effect of a prejudiced imagination; in cases, people relate first with an honest zeal to relate as an opinion, next as a matter of fact. The only material facts on which I would observe here, is the expression ascribed to the prisoner, of the Manhattan Well, but that circumstance will be satisfactorily accounted for, by proving to you that he had been previously informed that the muff had been found there, and it was therefore natural to enquire if the body was not found there also—If, gentlemen, we show you all this, you will be able to say, before leaving your seats, that there is nothing to warrant you in pronouncing the prisoner Guilty.

In this clever speech Burr used the public hostility to Levi against the prosecution, and implied that Elma was no better than she should be, while at the same time offering the suggestion that she was so morose over her "dependency" upon the Ring family that she could have drowned herself. Circumstances, he was saying, are often deceptive, and he called up before the jury the awful possibility of the death of an innocent man. The matter of the sleigh he discarded with contempt on the obvious fact that Mrs Broad was confused; he did not touch on the testimony of more reliable witnesses that they had seen a sleigh in the neighborhood of the Manhattan Well on that Sunday night.

The first witness for the defense was Demas Meed, Ezra Weeks's apprentice.

Defense: Do you live with Ezra Weeks, and did you the twenty-second of December last? Relate all you know.

Demas Meed: I live with Mr Ezra Weeks as an apprentice, and take care of his horse and sleigh. I lived with him in December last; I remember perfectly well taking care of the horse that night, and I either left the key after locking the gate as usual, on the mantelpiece, or I put it in my pocket. I can't say certainly which.

Question by one of the jury: Was it a weekday or on Sunday?

Demas Meed: On Sunday. I lock the gate every night—I locked it that night a little after dark, and before eight o'clock.

Jury or Defense(?): Did you miss the key in the morning?

Demas Meed: I did not.

Defense: If anybody had taken out the horse and sleigh for half an hour, should you not have known it?

Demas Meed: I don't know certainly as I should; the stable is some way from the house.

Defense: Did you see anything mislaid?

Demas Meed: Nothing.

Defense: Has the harness bells?

Demas Meed: It has eight, tied on in four places—there was no harness without bells.

Defense: Where was you that evening?

Demas Meed: I was the whole evening in the kitchen, except a little while when I was in the yard getting some wood.

Question by the Court: Were the bells tied on so that they could be taken off if you chose?

Demas Meed: They were so.

Defense(?): You observed nothing unusual about the horse in the morning, you say. He did not appear as if he had been used hard?

Demas Meed: I did not.

Question by one of the jury: When you saw the bells next day, were they tied as you left them?

Demas Meed: They seemed to be tied as I left them.

Question by Mr Colden: Did you take notice, do you remember whether they were tied by yourself or not?

The boardinghouse where Elma Sands lived until her disappearance on December 22, 1799. (Lithograph by Sarony, Major & Knapp for *Valentine's Manual* of 1861) Courtesy of the Museum of the City of New York.

Lispenard Meadows from a point on Broadway near Spring Street, the site of the Manhattan Well, where Elma's body was found. (Ink-wash by Alexander Anderson, 1798) Courtesy of the L.N. Phelps Stokes Collection, Miriam & Ira D. Wallach Division of Art, Prints and Photographs, The New York Public Library, Astor, Lenox and Tilden Foundations.

A typical winter street scene in a middle-class neighborhood near the Ring boardinghouse in old New York. (Watercolor by the Baroness Hyde de Neuville, 1809) Courtesy of the Museum of the City of New York.

The only known contemporary view of the Collect or Fresh Water Pond, the most important source of water for New York City in the early years of the Republic. (Engraving by Walter Aikman, 1798) Courtesy of the I.N. Phelps Stokes Collection, Miriam & Ira D. Wallach Division of Art, Prints and Photographs, The New York Public Library, Astor, Lenox and Tilden Foundations.

Portrait of Cadwallader D. Colden, by John Wesley Jarvis. Courtesy of The New-York Historical Society, New York City.

Portrait of Aaron Burr (1809), by John Vanderlyn. Courtesy of The New-York Historical Society, New York City.

Portrait of Alexander Hamilton, by John Trumbell. Courtesy of The New-York Historical Society, New York City.

Federal Hall, site of the trial of Levi Weeks, during the inauguration of Gen. George Washington, April 30, 1789. Courtesy of the Museum of the City of New York.

A view of the upper end of Broad Street, with City Hall at the end. (Watercolor drawing by George Holland, 1797) Courtesy of the I.N. Phelps Stokes Collection, Miriam & Ira D. Wallach Division of Art, Prints and Photographs, The New York Public Library, Astor, Lenox and Tilden Foundations.

Alexander Hamilton's home, The Grange, built by Ezra Weeks, the brother of the accused, and John McComb, a witness in the trial of Levi Weeks. (Lithograph by George Hayward for *Valentine's Manual* of 1858) Courtesy of The New-York Historical Society, New York City.

Richmond Hill, the home of Aaron Burr. (Lithograph from *Valentine's Manual* of 1856) Courtesy of the New-York Historical Society, New York City.

Aaron Burr and Alexander Hamilton face each other in a duel in Weehawken. (Wood engraving by P. Meeder from *Lamb's History of New York*, Vol. 2) Courtesy of The New-York Historical Society, New York City.

Demas Meed: I did not.

Mr Colden(?): How many minutes would it consume to take the bells off and put them on?

Demas Meed: Five or six.

Question by Mr Colden: If you had laid the key upon the mantelpiece, and some person had taken it off and put it there again after keeping it half an hour, might it not have been done without your knowledge?

Demas Meed: I don't know but that it might, but I don't think it could, for I was only once out of the kitchen to fetch an armful of wood.

Question by the Court: Were the sleigh and harness kept together?

Demas Meed: Yes.

Defense: How long would it take you to harness the horse and tackle the sleigh?

Demas Meed: About ten or fifteen minutes.

Defense: Did you see Levi Weeks that evening?

Demas Meed: Mr M'Combs and his wife were there—I don't exactly know what time they went away, but after they were gone a little time, I heard somebody go upstairs, about half an hour afterwards—a little before nine, I went upstairs and there I saw Mr Levi Weeks sitting.

Defense: Are you sure that no other person were in?

Demas Meed: Not to my knowledge.

This witness, although obviously disposed to help the defense, was vague enough about some points to raise questions. Mr Colden did not inquire into the confused time sequence: the apprentice did not know what time the McCombs went away, nor was he sure of the time then when he heard "somebody go upstairs"—about half an hour later, he thought. But he was specific that it was "a little before nine" when he saw Levi Weeks in the parlor. Most of the witnesses were agreed that they heard shrieks coming from the Well some time around nine o'clock. Demas Meed was providing Levi with an alibi.

The next witness was Lorena Forrest, a neighbor of the Rings.

Defense: Do you live near Mrs Ring's, Ma'am?

Lorena Forrest: I live next door.

Defense: Pray tell us what you know about this affair.

Lorena Forrest: It was about twelve o'clock, as near as I can recollect, on the second day of January, the day when she was found, that Levi Weeks came to our house to buy some tobacco. I asked him if there was any news of Elmore—he answered, no. I told him that I expected Ring's family had, for they seemed much agitated. He went away, and in about half an hour he came in again while we sat at table, about one o'clock—I had heard before this about the muff's being found; Mrs Ring had informed me—and I told him that Mrs Ring had mentioned to me that the muff and handkerchief had been found in a drain near Bayard's lane.

Defense: Did you take any particular notice of his countenance?

Lorena Forrest: I did—I did not perceive any change or alteration in it.

Question by one of the jury: Was the Manhattan Well mentioned?

Lorena Forrest: There was nothing said about the Manhattan Well.

This question, which we assume would have been asked by Mr Colden if a member of the jury had not anticipated him, elicited a response somewhat damaging to the defense. If the Manhattan Well were not mentioned in connection with the muff, why did Levi ask Mr Lent whether Elma's body had been found in the Well? Possibly an awareness of the need to distract the jury from this dangerous line of thought prompted the defense's next question.

Defense: Did you not hear Mr Croucher say, that he came near the Well the evening when she was missing?

Lorena Forrest: Yes, he told me he did, and said that he generally came that way.

Joseph Watkins, Elias Ring's next-door neighbor, was then sworn in. William Coleman says at this point that "this witness was present at the finding of the body, and he gave pretty nearly the same account with the other witnesses, excepting that when he came to describe the marks of violence appearing on the deceased, he said her socks and stockings were worn out on the ball of her foot and were entirely whole on the upper part—this he was positive of." This testimony of course conflicted with the description given by James W. Lent, who had said that Elma's stockings were torn at the toes, that her right foot was bare and scratched on the upper part, as though she had been dragged across the ground.

Defense: Do you remember anything in the conduct of Mr Ring that led you to suspicions of improper conduct between him and Elma?

This question must have come as a considerable shock to the people in the courtroom—not least of all to Catherine Ring.

Joseph Watkins: About the middle of September, Mrs Ring being in the country, I imagined one night I heard a shaking of a bed and considerable noise there, in the second story, where Elma's bed stood; the bed stood within four inches of the partition. I heard a man's voice, and a woman's. I am very positive that the voice was not Levi's.

Question by one of the jury: Could you hear through the partition?

Joseph Watkins: Pretty distinctly.

Defense: Did the noise of the bed continue any time?

Joseph Watkins: It continued some time and it must have been very loud to have awakened me. I heard a man's voice pretty loud and lively, and joking; the voice was loud and unguarded. I said to my wife,

> "It is Ring's voice," and I told my wife, "That girl will be ruined next." I felt a good deal hurt at the time, but never mentioned it or anything about it to anybody afterwards, till after Elma was lost.

Mr Colden, who had not objected to the speculation in the foregoing testimony, rose for cross-examination.

Mr Colden: When did you last see the front room in Ring's house, of which you speak?

Joseph Watkins: I do not know when.

Mr Colden: Have you been there lately?

Joseph Watkins: No.

Mr Colden: Were you there any time last fall?

Joseph Watkins: I cannot say I was.

Mr Colden: Have you ever seen the bed that stands there?

Joseph Watkins: I don't know that I have.

Mr Colden: You have said the bed was next to your room, how do you know this?

Joseph Watkins: I have seen the bed placed so.

Mr Colden did not explore this mystifying reply; how, if Mr Watkins didn't know that he had ever seen the bed, could he say he had seen the bed "placed?" Mr Colden did not dwell on this.

Mr Colden: What kind of partition is it which divides the houses?

Joseph Watkins: A plank partition, lathed and plastered both sides. I made it myself.

Mr Colden: Are you certain it was Ring's voice, sir?

Joseph Watkins: I took it to be Ring's.

Mr Colden: Could you distinguish the other to be a woman's voice?

Joseph Watkins: I could not certainly, because it was so low.

Mr Watkins was, in his way, as doubtful a witness as Susannah Broad. Mr Colden did not remind him of his testimony in which he said, "I heard a man's voice and a woman's."

Mr Colden: Did you ever hear anything before, that induced you to suspect that there was an improper connection between Mr Ring and Elma?

Joseph Watkins: I will not undertake, expressly, to say.

Mr Colden: When was this?

Joseph Watkins: A little after the middle of September.

This exchange is not clear, although it may have seemed clear to the prosecutor and the witness; the Court and the jury did not question it.

Mr Colden: How often have you heard this noise of the bed?

Joseph Watkins: From eight to fourteen times, in the time of the sickness.

Mr Colden: When did this occur, of which you particularly spoke?

Joseph Watkins: Possibly from the twentieth of September to October.

Mr Colden: Was this ever mentioned, do you say?

Joseph Watkins: Never out of the house till after the girl was missing.

Defense: Did you ever hear this noise after Mrs Ring came from the country?

Joseph Watkins: I never did.

Defense [It would seem that this was a defense question although it is identified only by "Q."]: Do you remember that Mrs Ring came into your house one morning, and what did she say?

Joseph Watkins: She came into our house one morning, and said Elmore was so sick since she was at your house last night, that we have all been employed to take care of her. My wife said, "She was not here." Mrs Ring said, "Aye, she told me she had been."

Defense: What character did Mrs Ring give of the prisoner?

Joseph Watkins: I heard her say, the Thursday after she was missing, that he was very kind and friendly to all the family, particularly when sick, but not more so to this girl than to the rest. He was more like one of the family than a boarder.

This testimony conflicts with the general tenor of Mrs Ring's attitude toward Levi Weeks after Elma's disappearance; Mr Colden however did not pursue this point but continued to dwell on the alleged affair between Elias Ring and Elma.

Mr Colden: Did you ever tell anybody that you thought the persons whom you overheard was Mr Ring and Elma?

Joseph Watkins: No.

Mr Colden: Did you ever speak of this noise which you and your wife heard in the night to anybody else?

Joseph Watkins: I don't know but I once said to Croucher that I believed he had a hand in it.

This surprising remark was not pursued by Mr Colden.

Defense: Did you ever converse with Croucher about where he was the evening Elma was missing?

Joseph Watkins: I asked him once where he was that evening, but do not know what answer he made.

Defense: Did you ever see Croucher busy in spreading suspicions against the prisoner?

Joseph Watkins: The day she was laid out in the street, I saw him very busy in attempting to make people believe the prisoner was guilty.

Mr Colden: When did you first mention to Croucher what you heard in the chamber?

Joseph Watkins: At the Coroner's Jury.

Mr Colden: How could you distinguish between the voice of Mr Ring and Mr Weeks?

Joseph Watkins: Ring's is a high sounding voice; that of Weeks a low soft voice.

Mrs Watkins' deposition was then read into the record. This deposition Coleman says was taken, as we have seen, on the first day of the trial by Mr Colden, Judge Lansing and Hamilton, because her breasts were very "sore and festered" and she was consequently too ill to come into court. However, the official court minutes say that the deposition was taken on the second day of the trial, after the close of the prosecution's case. The Hamilton scholar, Julius Goebel Jr, believes that the deposition had to have been taken on the second day, because the defense lawyers would not have allowed Colden to find out about this testimony earlier. They were far too clever to miss an opportunity to catch their opponent off guard. Goebel points to Colden's obvious annoyed confusion during his cross-examination of Joseph Watkins as proof that Watkins' testimony had taken the Assistant Attorney General by surprise.[46]

Mrs Watkins was asked, "Did Catherine Ring inform you anything respecting Levi Weeks's character and his behaviour in the family, and especially as to any person sick?"

Mrs Watkins replied, "On Thursday evening, after Miss Sands was missing, Mrs Ring came to see this deponent and, in conversation, said that Levi Weeks was one of the best, most civil, and kind-hearted boarders that she ever had, and if any of the children were sick, he was a kind and attentive to them as if they were his own, and was remarkably affectionate and kind to them on the slightest complaint they made; and that his behaviour was invariably that of an amiable and obliging person."

This statement is in direct conflict with Mrs Ring's testimony at the beginning of the trial:

Defense: Did you never say that Levi was very attentive to your children or any in your family, when they were sick?

Catherine Ring: I never did. I could not, for none of my children ever was sick while he was in the house.

Mr Colden did not challenge the deposition. The next witness was Captain A. Rutgers:

Captain Rutgers: I remember very well meeting Mr Ring one day, on Sunday afternoon; he asked me if I had heard of a muff's being found anywhere? I replied it was an odd question. He said they were looking for a young woman who was missing, a relation of his wife's, and she had been gone a week. I asked him what he supposed had become of her; either he or some person with him, said they had reason to believe she was drowned, and they supposed it was a love fit. I advised them to employ Mr G. Walgrove, who was an expert person at sweeping the river on such occasions. From what passed at that time I had no idea that Mr Ring then thought she was murdered.

This testimony elicited no questions. Lorena Forrest, the Rings' neighbor, was recalled.

Defense: Have you had at any time any conversation with Croucher, and what was it?

Lorena Forrest: A day or two after Elma was found, he was at our house, and he said it was a very unfortunate thing that he had not come that way just at the time, as he might have saved her life. He said he had come by that night.

Defense: You are very well persuaded he said this?

Lorena Forrest: I am, very well.

This question, put obviously for its rhetorical effect, apparently moved the Assistant Attorney General to cross-examination. He seems to have lost his temper.

Mr Colden: Repeat the terms of the conversation.

Lorena Forrest: After the young woman had been found and after the jury had sat—

Mr Colden: That is fifteen days after she was lost. Give us the very terms, Ma'am, if you please.

Lorena Forrest: Upon my telling him what he had sworn before the Grand Jury—

Mr Colden: You mean the Coroner's Jury.

Lorena Forrest: —he said he did come along there that evening, but not at that hour.

Mr Colden(?): Did he then say anything about Mrs Brown, or Mrs Ashmore's house?

Lorena Forrest: He did not say anything about any house.

Mr Watkins' daughter, Betsy, was the next witness for the defense. She was asked whether she knew Elma Sands.

Betsy Watkins: Yes, I knew her very well, for we live next door.

Defense: Do you know which was her bedroom?

Betsy Watkins: She had a front bedchamber which was against my mother's; I know because I used to sit out upon the stoop late at night, and when she went to bed she frequently used to hold the candle out of the window.

Defense: Do you remember Mrs Ring's coming into your house and speaking about Elma's being out at nights?

Betsy Watkins: I remember that Mrs Ring came to our house one morning and said her boarders had gone out without breakfast—that Elma had been sick all night, ever since she came from our house, and she thought it arose from her sitting over our stove. My mother replied that she had not been at our house—"then," said Mrs Ring, "perhaps she had been at Mr Forrest's."

Defense: Have you ever heard Mrs Ring say anything of the prisoner's behaviour in the family?

Betsy Watkins: I heard her say one day, I think it was Wednesday, after Elma was missing, that he was very kind and attentive to the family; if any of the children had the least complaint in the world, he was very attentive to them.

Defense: Did Mrs Ring say anything about the appearance of Elma the day of the twenty-second, and what was it?

Betsy Watkins: She said that in the evening Elma went upstairs, and she followed her up with a candle, or went up, I can't say which. She fixed her handkerchief at the glass. She said that Elma looked pale, and she told her not to be frightened—"No," she said, and she came down and leaned her head upon her hand—she said she thought she afterwards heard a whispering in the entry.

The Watkins family were united in the defense cause. Betsy's testimony that Catherine Ring had said that she found Elma pale and frightened on that Sunday night conflicted with the testimony of Elizabeth Osborn who had said she "seemed very lively and very happy." Mr Colden did not remind the jurors of Elizabeth Osborn's testimony. Further he did not attempt to elicit information about Betsy's relationship with Elma, nor her opinion of her.

Dr Prince was called, to rebut conclusions drawn by physicians testifying for the prosecution.

Dr Prince: I was called upon by a constable to attend the coroner's jury which was sitting on the body of Elma Sands. When I came in, I saw the body lying on the table before the jury; I proceeded to examine it. I saw some scratches and a small bruise on the knee. The body was then dissected—saw no extravasations of blood—I saw no spots about the neck—I saw a little spot upon the breast, which I could cover with my thumb—I saw no marks of violence—I saw no appearances but what might be accounted for by supposing she drowned herself.*

Defense: Did you particularly examine the neck?

Dr Prince: Not more than any other part.

Defense: If there had been any very remarkable spots, would you not have seen them?

Dr Prince: I should—I examined particularly—I was called for that purpose.

Question by the Court: Did you see no bruise on the breast?

Dr Prince: I saw a small contusion.

Defense: Was the neck broken?

Dr Prince: It was not, nor was there any dislocation.

Dr Prince's testimony was corroborated by another physician named Mackintosh.

Dr Mackintosh: I was called upon together with Dr Prince, on the third of January last to attend a

*The coroner's inquest on the body extended from Friday morning, January 3, until the next night.

coroner's inquest on the body of Elma Sands, and I was desired particularly, by the jury, to examine and see if she was pregnant. There were no marks of violence—and we discovered, to the satisfaction of the jury, that she was not pregnant. It was suggested by some of the jury that her neck was broke: I examined and found it was not, neither was the collarbone dislocated. The scarf skin of the face was scratched as with gravel—near the instep there was a small spot like a blood blister. It seemed as if the knee had been injured by falling upon coarse gravel—there was a spot upon the breast, but there were no marks of violence upon the belly—I think there were not marks of violence sufficient to cause her death.

I have been in the custom of seeing numbers of drowned people who have been brought to the Alms-House, and have often seen livid spots upon the skin, much such as I saw in this instance. I took it to be the effect of suffocation rather than anything else.

The Assistant Attorney General cross-examined Dr Mackintosh.

Mr Colden: Would that produce a row of spots around the neck?

Dr Mackintosh: Why, if the body was gangrened it would be no matter—it might or it might not.

Question by the Court: If the hand had been hurt by a blow, would you have seen and noticed it?

Dr Mackintosh: I should.

Mr Colden: Was there any water in the body?

Dr Mackintosh: A small quantity, but very little is sufficient to drown—there might have been a quart.

Question by one of the jury: Would a spoonful drown?

Dr Mackintosh: Yes, unless it could be thrown up by the effect of cough.

Mr Colden: Suppose she had been killed first, and then thrown into the Well, would the body have any water in it?

Dr Mackintosh: It might.

Question by Defense: Is it your opinion, sir, from all you saw, that the death was occasioned by drowning?

Dr Mackintosh: It is.

A third doctor, Dr Romayne, was called by the defense.

Dr Romayne: I cannot undertake to give any decided opinion upon appearances without seeing the body. Persons will vary extremely in the accounts they give, as well as in the conclusions they draw from appearances. The impressions upon the senses are in many cases remarkably nice and cannot be described, from the poverty of language, so as to convey correct ideas to others. An experienced

> person of good judgment might perhaps discover, upon inspection, whether bruises made upon the body were done before or after death. A body which had been taken out of the water would assume a different appearance from what it had at first, in ten minutes after it was exposed to air, and every day the appearance of injury done would acquire more visibility as it advanced in putrefaction. I have examined many bodies after death by hanging and never could discover that the red color of the countenance was materially changed from what it was in life or just before sudden death. Pressure upon the veins so as to interrupt the circulation will give a blue or black tint or florid appearance; pressure upon the arteries is likely to produce paleness.

This testimony caused great confusion in the minds of the Court and the jurors. The question that immediately arises is why, if the two physicians who dissected the body for the coroner's jury both believed that Elma had drowned herself and there were no marks of violence upon her, did the coroner's jury bring in a verdict of "MURDER by some person or persons yet unknown?"[47]

The great age of medical discovery lay decades ahead; at this time medical quackery was commonplace. Before the Revolution, there were only two medical schools in the colonies: one in Philadelphia and the other at King's College, later Columbia, in New York City. After Independence, efforts were being made to upgrade medical training; most American doctors had studied at European schools or had been trained in this country under the apprentice system. Public sentiment however, was adamantly opposed to the dissection of cadavers for purposes of medical education.

Coroners at this time were seldom doctors, and the coroner's jury was made up of the coroner's friends and acquaintances; since this was a service for which the jurors were paid, it was much sought after. Dr Milton Helpern has written that until the twentieth century a candidate for coroner had to meet only one qualification: he had to prove that he had never been in prison. Dr Helpern found decisions in early coroner's cases to be so often "blatantly wrong" that, apart from "sheer ineptitude" only bribery could be responsible.[48]

In this case the presence of two doctors on the coroner's jury reflected a special effort. Examination of Elma's body had supposedly lasted for two days, and now the physicians were giving evidence that appeared to contradict their own coroner's verdict, and that certainly contradicted the testimony of the prosecution's medical witnesses. The most respected of these was Dr David Hosack. He was consequently recalled to the stand and asked, possibly by the Court, whether there was "any way in which the testimony we have heard can be reconciled?"

Dr Hosack: I think it may in either of two ways. First, the spots might not have been, and I presume were not, as visible at the time the body was first taken out of the water as after it had been exposed to the air for some days. This change of color in bruises is not uncommon in the living body, and I presume somewhat similar colors may occur by the process of putrefaction after death. At first there may be very little change of color in the injured part, but, after some time, it undergoes a very considerable alteration.

Secondly, it occurs to me that it was supposed that the neck and collarbone were broken when she was first taken out of the Well, and as I did not see her until the day of interment, it is possible that the frequent turning and bending the head, and the frequent examination of the neck to ascertain the injury done to the collarbone, may have produced the appearance on the neck I before mentioned, especially as the body had been dead for several days, and the vessels had become tender; in which case, very little violence might have produced an effusion of blood under the skin.

These circumstances I did not advert to in my examination in the morning, not knowing the injury done to the neck and collarbone, which have been since related.

Question by the Court(?): How much water will the lungs take in after death?

Dr Hosack: Only as much as the windpipe will hold can be received. The lungs collapse at the last expiration, and a very inconsiderable quantity of water can be received afterwards. But this I do not assert from my own knowledge of the state of the body after death by drowning, but upon the authority of Dr Coleman, of London, who asserts that he frequently observed this fact upon dissection.

After the body has lain a long time under water, it is not unusual to find water in it.

Thus Dr Hosack attempted to save face, so to speak, for the medical community. He was not asked to explain, of course, why the coroner's physicians had brought in a verdict of murder when they now appeared to think Elma committed suicide. He did not say that he himself no longer believed that Elma had been murdered.

The defense next called David Forest, who was asked if "he knew anything about Croucher, the witness."

David Forest: On the twenty-sixth of December last, Croucher came to my store to buy a loaf of bread. He said Ring's family were in great distress, and it was nothing strange to him after what his landlord had said, and being under the same roof it gave him great uneasiness. His own opinion, he said, was that the girl had made way with herself.

On Friday last Croucher came running into the store and said, "What do you think of this innocent young man now? There is material evidence against him from the Jerseys, and he is taken by the High Sheriff, sir, and carried to jail; he will be carried from there, sir, to the court and be tried; from there he will be carried back to jail, and from thence to court again, sir, and from thence to the place of execution, and there be hanged by the neck until he is dead."

Defense: Did he say this in an angry tone?

David Forest: I can't say it was anger or not; he has a quick way of speaking.

Defense: Had he any particular business with you at this time?

David Forest: He did not seem to have any but to tell me this.

Ezra Lacey was called.

Ezra Lacey: I was a lodger in the house of Mrs Ring and was there the night she was missing. Levi Weeks was there about eight o'clock in the evening. I felt unwell and I came in about eight o'clock. I remember Russel, who was with me, took out his watch and said it was two minutes before, or two minutes after eight, I can't say which.

We sat a while, and he then took out his watch again and said it was ten minutes after eight; after this—not long, perhaps five or six minutes—we got up and went to bed and left Mr Ring and this young man and Elma there together—I don't know whether Mrs Ring was there or not.

Defense: Did you observe any change in his countenance or behavior after Elma was missing?

Presumably this question referred to Levi Weeks.

Ezra Lacey: None, not the least.

Defense: Did you observe any particular attention by the prisoner to Elma?

Ezra Lacey: I had lodged in the house only five or six days before the twenty-second of December, but I thought he was more attentive to Hope than to Elma.

Defense: Did you ever hear any threats against the prisoner by Ring?

Ezra Lacey: I was once in company one evening, and Ring was there, and I heard somebody say if Levi Weeks should get clear by law, it would not be safe for him to appear in public, and Ring said he thought so too.

Defense: Did you not hear threats from Ring himself?

Ezra Lacey: I heard Ring say that if he should meet him in the dark, he should not think it wrong to put him a' one side if he had a loaded pistol, if he thought he should not be found out in it. I went to the door pretty soon after, and Mr Van Alstine followed me. I told him I was really surprised that Ring should express himself in this manner. He said he thought so too.

Mr Van Alstine was later to call this testimony into question.

During the testimony of the next witness, William Dustan, the defense staged a dramatic bit of business which was to give rise to some garbled reports of the trial.

William Dustan: Last Friday morning, a man, I don't know his name, came into my store—

Here, Coleman says, "one of the prisoner's counsel held a candle close to Croucher's face, who stood among the crowd, and asked the witness if it was he and he said it was."

William Dustan: He said, "Good morning, gentlemen, Levi Weeks is taken up by the High Sheriff and there is fresh evidence against him from Hackensack." He then went away and as he went out, he said, "My name is Croucher," and that is all the business he had with me.

It is not clear which member of the defense team held the candle to Croucher's face: both Hamilton and Burr apparently claimed credit for doing it, although the story gained much in the telling. James Parton, Aaron Burr's biographer, wrote in 1858 that Burr held two candelabra before Croucher's face and cried, "Behold the murderer, gentlemen!" The flickering lights playing over Croucher's unlovely features created, Parton says, a ghastly effect, and Croucher fled the room in terror.[49]

Hamilton's family maintained that it was Hamilton who held candles—and not candelabra—to Croucher's face. Hamilton's widow always said it was her husband who did it, and John Church Hamilton, the statesman's son, wrote a vivid description of what is surely an apochryphal event; he said that because of strong public prejudice against Levi Weeks, his defense loomed as a "herculean task." The courtroom was pervaded with "a dark and sullen animosity" because it was feared that Hamilton's talents would get Weeks off. Hamilton's "logical powers" had convinced him that Croucher had murdered Elma, so when Croucher was called to the witness stand the defense lawyer placed a candle on each side of the man so that the light would shine on his face, and "fixed on him a piercing eye." The prosecution objected, but Hamilton responded "in the deepest tones of his voice, 'I have special reasons, reasons that when the real culprit is detected and placed before the Court, will be understood.' "

While the spectators "bent forward in breathless anxiety," Hamilton said: " 'The Jury will mark every muscle of his face, every motion of his eye. I conjure you to look through that man's countenance to his conscience.' " Fixed with the piercing eye, Croucher, under questioning, "plunged from one admission to another, from contradiction to contradiction" and when at last he left the stand, "the spectators turned from him in horror."[50]

Hamilton's grandson, Allan McLane Hamilton, attempted to tone down this flamboyant story by saying that his grandfather held the candle to Croucher's face only for illumination, because daylight was waning, and he needed light so that Croucher could be identified.[51]

None of these fanciful events found its way into the reports of Coleman or Hardie, for the very good reason that they did not happen. All this embroidery obviously stemmed from "the prisoner's counsel"—and we cannot tell whether this was Burr or Hamilton—holding a candle near Croucher's face as he stood among the spectators and asking William Dustan if this was the man who had come into his store and said that Levi Weeks had been arrested, which indeed he had been. This theatrical byplay was intended to associate Croucher in the minds of the jury with guilt, although the action described by Mr Dustan demonstrated at worst a kind of mean-spirited self-importance; at best it revealed Croucher to be a gossip.

It was not difficult for the defense to find people who disliked Croucher. Another one was Hugh McDougall.

Hugh McDougall: I had been acquainted with Mr Croucher for some time, but I never liked his looks. On the second of January, the day when the

> body was found, he was extremely busy among the crowd to spread improper insinuations and prejudices against the prisoner, who was then taken; and among other things he told a story about his losing a pocket book. This conduct I thought unfair and I told him so plainly.
>
> "O but," says he, "there's the story of the pocket book—" and stopped there.
>
> He used to bring several articles of wearing apparel such as shawls and so forth to dispose of, but I noticed that he always managed so as to come just at dinner time—I told my wife that I did not like the man and desired that she would tell him that in future if he wanted anything of me, that I would call on him. Last Monday, while I was busy in my garden, he came again.
>
> "Now," says he, "the thing has all come out, the thing is settled, there is point blank proof come from the Jerseys of a new fact."
>
> I told him I thought it wrong and highly improper that he should persecute Weeks in such a manner when he had a difference with him; that for my own part, I wanted some further evidence before I should condemn the man.

The reference to the Jerseys involved a rumor which was circulating that a New Jersey man had come forward and confessed to having been an accessory to the murder and was willing to testify at the trial.

Mr Colden apparently did not attempt to interrupt this stream of insinuations and prejudices against Mr Croucher, whose words and demeanor on the stand had certainly been that of a perfect villain and who even, oddly enough, had a suitable surname for villainy.

The defense called another of Mr Ring's erstwhile lodgers. His name was Timothy B. Crane.

Timothy Crane: I lodged at Mr Ring's a fortnight, about a week or eight days before the girl was missing.

Defense: Did you observe any particular attention from the prisoner to Elma?

Timothy Crane: I thought he paid as much attention to Hope as to her.—I left the house on the fourteenth of December.

Defense: What was Elma's temper when you was there—was she unusually gay?

Timothy Crane: She seemed of a melancholy make; sometimes she would pass a joke, but it seemed forced.

Defense: Had you any opportunity of examining the countenance and conduct of Levi?

Timothy Crane: On Wednesday after she was missing, I was told that Levi was suspected, and that it would be his ruin. I observed particularly after that, his countenance and behaviour; I could not see that there was the least difference in either. He laid out the work of the shop as usual. I inquired

> of my friends every day, and was told that things grew worse and worse, suspicions rose higher and I watched him closer, but I never discovered the least alteration.

It is interesting that in the ensuing cross-examination, Mr Colden did not ask Mr Crane how he earned his living, since it would appear from the statement, "He laid out the work of the shop as usual," that Timothy Crane was also an employee of Ezra Weeks; if this were so, it might offer a reason to the jury for his opinion of Elma's disposition, which differed so widely from the jolly, pleasant one described by the prosecution witnesses. But Mr Colden did not bring this up.

> *Mr Colden:* How long was Elma sick while you were there?
>
> *Timothy Crane:* Nearly half the time.
>
> *Mr Colden:* Was not her melancholy owing to her sickness?
>
> *Timothy Crane:* No.

Mr Colden did not ask Mr Crane how he knew this, since he had been in the Ring household only two weeks; and by asking about her "melancholy" he appeared to accept that she *was* melancholy.

> *Question by Defense:* Did you never see her take unusual quantities of laudanum?
>
> *Timothy Crane:* I was there one evening and Dr Snedecher was present; she asked him for

laudanum, and he offered to give her some if she would let him drop it into her mouth, which she consented to, and he dropt a number of drops into her mouth which surprised us all. She said she wished she had a phial full; she would take it.

Mr Colden: Did Mrs Ring ever tell you that she never saw Elma after she went upstairs?

Timothy Crane: I understood that she never saw her after she went upstairs; I will not be very positive, but it is still my belief.

Question by the Court: Did she speak of her adjusting her shawl?

Timothy Crane: I think she put it on below.

The defense called John McComb, the architect who was to design Hamilton's house, The Grange, which was built by Ezra Weeks. Coleman calls him "John B. Combs."

Defense: Do you remember anything that happened the evening that Elma was missing?

John McComb: Between six and seven o'clock on the twenty-second of December, my wife and myself went to the house of Ezra Weeks; when we came in we found Levi sitting there, and he remained until eight o'clock. He conversed as usual, and when he got up to go away, he stood leaning for a minute upon the back of a chair, and then bid us good night. He appeared in no hurry to go at all.

Question by one of the jury: How did you know it was eight o'clock?

John McComb: We went from Ezra Weeks's to Henry Clements, where we stayed about twenty minutes.

Defense: How far is that?

John McComb: A few minutes walk only—It was eight o'clock as near as I can judge.

Defense: How long did you remain at Ezra Weeks's?

John McComb: About twenty or twenty-five minutes.

Defense: What time did you get home?

John McComb: It was a little after nine.

Defense: Why are you so particular in your recollection?

John McComb: Because Henry Clements came to me the Wednesday after she was missing, to ask if I could remember who was at Ezra Weeks's with me that Sunday evening, for although it might seem odd, yet I should hear more of it.

The difficulty here of course was the attempt of the defense to pin down the time that Levi left his brother's house on that Sunday evening, and the time that he returned. Mr McComb says that Levi left at eight o'clock; he cannot say what time he returned except that he was not back before they themselves left—after eight-thirty, if they stayed at Henry Clements' only twenty minutes or so, and were home "a little after nine."

The deposition of Elizabeth Weeks, Ezra Weeks's wife, was read; no reason was given for her absence from court:

Elizabeth Weeks, wife of Ezra Weeks, of the city of New-York, being duly sworn, saith, that on Sunday, the 22nd day of December last, she and her husband were at home. That about candle light, or a little while after, Mr John McCombs and his wife came in, that Levi Weeks (the person charged with the murder of Julianna Elmore [sic] Sands), was then in the room, and remained with the company till after the house clock struck eight, and then went away; that to the best of this deponent's knowledge and belief, Mr and Mrs McCombs left the house about twenty or twenty-five minutes after eight by the house clock; that after her husband had lighted Mr and Mrs McCombs out, and had returned into the room, before he had time to sit down, the said Levi Weeks came in, and remained with them, conversing on the business to be performed the next day—appeared cheerful, eat a hearty supper, and went off to his lodgings, as she believes, about ten o'clock; and that he appeared as cheerful as usual—she saw no particular difference in his conduct or behaviour.

Elizabeth Weeks

Sworn, this 18th day of January, 1800 before me Richard Harison, Recorder of New-York.

Demas Meed, Ezra Weeks's apprentice, was recalled.

Defense: Do you remember any thing about Mr and Mrs McCombs and his wife being at Ezra Weeks's on the twenty-second of December?

Demas Meed: Yes, I remember very well that I heard Mr Ezra Weeks say at the door, "hand a candle." After Mr McCombs was gone, I heard somebody go upstairs and in about half an hour I went up and found Mr Levi Weeks sitting there.

Ezra Weeks was called to the stand, where he delivered an elaborate statement which basically corroborated his wife's deposition.

Ezra Weeks: On Sunday, the twenty-second of December, my brother Levi came to my house about nine o'clock in the morning. I went to church and left him there. I dined that day at my father-in-law's, and did not return home till about five o'clock in the afternoon. Just as we had drank tea and were yet sitting at the table before we lit candles, my brother came in, and I believe in about half an hour afterwards Mr and Mrs McCombs came in, and my brother tarried till about eight o'clock, whether a little before or a little after I cannot say. Mr McCombs and his wife sat about twenty minutes as near as I can judge after my brother went out, I lighted them downstairs and held the candle to light them all the way to Mr Rhinelander's corner, it being very slippery and dark, cautioned them to take care.

I came up again—just as I sit down the candle, before I had time to sit down myself, Levi my brother came in to enquire about the business of the next day, as he had the charge of my shop, understanding the business as well as myself, and very attentive to it, I am seldom at the shop more than once a day. I attended to the business abroad, took dimensions of work on my memorandum, and gave it to my brother in writing—his business was to give directions to the journeymen for execution—Here is eight doors on my memorandum—

He showed it to the Court and the jury.

—of different dimensions for Mr James Cumming's house, which he took down that evening on a piece of paper as I called them off: he gave directions to the journeymen for their execution—the doors was made without any mistake, fitted for their designed places, and without any further directions from me.

It was a general practice of my brother's to call on me of an evening to consult me about business of next the next day, and if company happened to interfere, if he did not stay till the company was gone, he seldom failed to come in again before he went to bed. That night he came accordingly, he eat a hearty supper, he was as cheerful as ever I saw him, tarried till about ten o'clock and I suppose, went home as usual.

Defense: Did your brother inform you that the muff and handkerchief were found prior to his arrest?

Ezra Weeks: On the second day of January last, about two o'clock in the afternoon, I was sitting down to dinner and Levi came and told me that Mrs Forrest had told him that the muff and handkerchief was found in a well near Bayard's lane. I told him that it must be the Manhattan Well.

It will be remembered that Mrs Forrest, in her testimony, actually said she told Levi that the items had been found in a *drain* near Bayard's lane, and she answered specifically, "Nothing was said about the Manhattan Well."

Question by Mr Colden: How came you to mention the Manhattan Well?

Ezra Weeks: The reason why the Manhattan Well came first to my recollection, was that I had furnished the wood materials for that Well, and as my business often called me that way, I rode past the Well almost every day.

Question by either Mr Colden or Defense: Did your brother know where the Well was?

Ezra Weeks: I believe he knew the situation to the Well.

Question by Mr Colden(?): Had he not been there before the arrest?

Ezra Weeks: Not to my knowledge. I do not think he was there until his arrest. I understood him that he was never there before the officer took him there, but I am not certain.

The defense next called Charles Thurston, an employee of Ezra Weeks, and asked him, "Are you acquainted with Mr Levi Weeks?"

Charles Thurston: It is about two years since I first worked there, first in the capacity of a journeyman, then as a foreman. I was there about Christmas. There was a rumour in the shop that Miss Elma Sands was missing. Mr Levi Weeks then kept the books, and they were kept just as well as they had been before, and his conduct was as usual. From the time the girl was missing I never saw any difference in his conduct.

The defense called Peter Fenton and Joseph Hall for the purpose of estimating the distance from the Ring house to the Manhattan Well "by Greenwich-street . . . they testified that it was 79 chains, that is, a mile wanting 22 yards. The distance by Broadway and Barley-street is greater. The last witness added, that he had made the experiment to see how short a time a horse might be drove from Rings' to the Manhattan Well and back again, and found it fifteen minutes. He gave the prisoner a good character."

This testimony was a response to testimony by the prosecution witness, Mr Williams, who had said that he had driven a horse from the Ring house to the Manhattan Well, and from there back to Ezra Weeks's down Barley Street in bad weather, and it had taken no more than sixteen minutes. Since both witnesses agreed, the defense testimony seems superfluous.

At this point Mr Colden addressed the Court for the second time on the admissibility as evidence of the deceased's remarks. He said he was not attempting to question the Court's judgment, but the case had now taken on a new aspect: "it had now been made a point of defense, that the mind of the deceased was melancholy and deranged—he thought the words as well as the look and behaviour of the deceased, should be given in evidence, it being equally an index of the mind and disposition and that in his opinion, this was the only way to arrive at truth."

Colonel Burr rose to argue against the Assistant Attorney General's position, but the Court told him not to bother; they said Mr Colden's statement did not sway them. His request was rejected.

Elias Ring was called back.

Defense: What time did you direct the docks to be dragged?

Elias Ring: I believe it was the first Sunday after she was missing.

Defense: What induced you to do this?

Elias Ring: I looked in the nearest dock because I heard that Ezra Weeks had declared that his brother had been absent about fifteen minutes, and therefore I supposed her drowned. We swept near Rhinelander's battery because I thought it was the handiest place, and being a byeplace, I thought it the most likely.

Defense: Is it a noted place?

Elias Ring: Pretty much so behind the battery.

The defense called Frederick Rhinelander.

Defense: Do you know the prisoner at the bar, and what character does he bear?

Frederick Rhinelander: I have known him some time, and have always considered him an industrious, active young man.

He went on to say that "at the request of David Hitchcock, on behalf of the prisoner, he had walked on Saturday last from Ring's to the Manhattan Well, and it took twenty minutes. He had done it a second time, when it took him twenty minutes to go and fifteen to return."

Defense: Is not the road to the Well a very rough and dangerous road?

Frederick Rhinelander: Yes.

Defense: Should you suppose that any person could drive a sleigh or carriage there in a dark night at all?

Frederick Rhinelander: No, I should not.

This bit of leading was ignored by the prosecution, although it was obvious from the discovery of sleigh tracks that a sleigh *had* been driven to the Well. The question could exist, of course, whether it had been driven at night.

Ezra Weeks was recalled, and asked if he knew whether his horse and sleigh had been out that Sunday evening. He replied, "I had no charge of my horse, my apprentice took care of him. I did not see him once a fortnight, I do not know as he had him that night."

The defense next called four character witnesses for Levi Weeks. Jonathan Burral, cashier of the Bank of New York, said that the summer before last the Directors of the Bank had hired Ezra Weeks to build a home in which the Cashier was at present living; it was his responsibility to protect the Bank from burglars day and night. Ezra

Weeks was rarely at the site, and the main burden of directing the work fell upon Levi Weeks whom the witness considered "a very industrious, prudent, civil and obliging young man," whose conduct "impressed the witness with a favourable opinion of his morals and his temper."

Then Philip Arcularius said he had known Levi for five years and agreed with Mr Burral's opinion of him. Thomas Ash had also known him four or five years, and "always remarked him for his modest and prudent behaviour." Mr McComb, as might be expected, "considered the prisoner a man of a very tender disposition." And finally, William Plimart gave a favorable opinion of Levi, saying "he was of a very mild temper."

This closed the case for the defense. The Assistant Attorney General now called a few more witnesses for the People.

The first of these prosecution witnesses was a man named Matthew Mustee.

Matthew Mustee: I saw a young man the Sunday-week before the girl was missing with a pole in his hand—

He was interrupted by the defense counsel.

Defense: Do you know Levi Weeks? Should you know the person you speak of if you saw him?

Matthew Mustee: I don't know as I should.

Mr Colden: Take the candle and look round and see if you can pick him out.

He went nearer the prisoner and pointed to him, saying that was he.

Defense: Will you undertake to swear that is the man you saw at the Well?

The witness had not had time even to mention the Well, but the aggressive approach of the defense counsel made him uncertain.

Matthew Mustee: I cannot swear to him.

Mr Colden: Well, sir, tell what you saw—

Matthew Mustee: The Sunday before the young woman was missing, I saw a young man sounding the Manhattan Well with a pole. I went up to him and asked him what he was about. He said he made the carpenter's work, and that he wanted to know the depth of the water. He measured it in different places and found it five foot five inches, five eight inches, and six foot.

Mr Colden: How was this man dressed?

Matthew Mustee: He had on a blue coatee, red jacket, blue breeches and white stockings.

Elias Ring was called back and asked if the prisoner ever wore these kind of clothes. He said he had never seen him wear a red jacket.

Mr Colden, weary, and undoubtedly seeing the handwriting on the wall, said, "If the court please we give up this point."

He called next character witnesses for Elias Ring, whose reputation had been under what can only be described as vicious attacks. The first witness, George Fleming, said he had known Elias Ring for five or six years at West-Point, and he had borne the character of a "man of credit."

Richardson Underhill, the second witness, also gave Elias Ring a good character, and testified further that Elma had a cheerful disposition and was good company—although he had not seen her for the past six months.

The third character witness for Elias Ring was Henry Clement, the man whom the McCombs had visited that Sunday night after they left the Weeks's, and who had approached John McComb the following Wednesday and warned him to "remember" who had been with him at Weeks's that night, "for he should hear more of it."

Clement gave Ring a good character and said that as far as he knew Ring was respected among the Friends and he too said that Elma had a lively, cheerful disposition.

Mr Colden: Do you recollect anything about Mr McComb coming to your house one Sunday evening?

Henry Clement: Yes, I remember his coming in on a Sunday evening, which I found afterwards as the same on which Elma Sands was missing. He and his wife came in, and he observed it was rather late to visit a neighbour—he said it was nine o'clock, or about nine o'clock—at any rate nine o'clock was somehow mentioned.

Mr Colden: Do you know what time it was yourself?

Henry Clement: I do not.

Mr Colden: How long did they stay?

Henry Clement: Not half an hour I am sure, and I don't think it was half the time.

If in fact Mr McComb had mentioned that he knew it was nine o'clock, a late time to be visiting, then his statement about leaving the Weeks house at eight-thirty was at best mistaken. The McCombs themselves could not have arrived at their own home much before nine-twenty. And Levi Weeks had not yet returned to his brother's house by close on nine o'clock. But Mr Clement himself did not know what time it was, and in any case it was late in the day for the prosecution to make this point.

Matthew Van Alstine was called, to comment on the testimony by Ezra Lacey for the defense. Mr Lacey had said that Elias Ring had said he would shoot Levi Weeks, "if he thought he should not be found out"—an odd remark for a Quaker to make. And Lacey had said this was in his own presence and in Matthew Van Alstine's presence. "I told [Mr Van Alstine] I was really surprised Ring should express himself in this manner," Ezra Lacey had said. "He said he thought so too."

Mr Colden: Did Ezra Lacey ever ask you or say anything to you about an observation of Ring, respecting the prisoner?

Matthew Van Alstine: One evening Ezra Lacey asked me if I did not hear Mr Ring say he would shoot Weeks? He related the circumstances—I made no answer; he said he thought it was very wrong in Mr Ring—I said I thought so too, but to say that I heard Mr Ring say so, I never did. It is possible it might have been said and I not hear it.

Again, this rebuttal of a defense witness was late in coming. And in fact the whole issue was an example of expert muddying of the waters by the defense, since anything Elias Ring said could have no bearing on whether or not Levi Weeks killed Elma Sands. Mr Ring himself did not go out that evening.

Another witness, John Willis, gave Elias Ring a good character and testified that Elma was cheerful and lively, as did Eleaser Ball, John Burk and Nathaniel Ring.

Catherine Ring was recalled once more by the prosecution. She was asked whether Elma was in the habit of staying out at night.

"She never was to my knowledge," said Catherine Ring, "never so as to alarm me." She was obviously still angry about words having been put in her mouth by the Watkinses, because she added, "And as to his kindness to my children, I must contradict that—as to the rest, it may be true, for he ever appeared of a tender disposition."

Mr Colden: Did you not say that you went to the front door that evening?

Catherine Ring: The moment Levi came in, I got up and went to the front door that he should not suspect me of knowing what Elma had told me.

A woman identified as "Ann Brown or Ann Ashmore" was called as a witness to Mr Croucher's whereabouts on the night in question.

Ann Brown/Ashmore: On the twenty-second day of December, being my little boy's birthday, I invited some of my friends to come and sup with me, and among the rest Mr Croucher. This was between twelve and one o'clock—accordingly between four and five o'clock in the evening he came and remained there till four or five minutes after eleven.

Mr Colden: Could he have been absent twenty minutes during that time?

Ann Brown/Ashmore: No, he was not.

Four more witnesses were called—Mary Searing, Ann Farrel, Jacob Hopper and Jeffrey Meeks. All testified "that they supped with Mrs Brown on the occasion of the birthday of her son, and that Croucher was of the party, and that he came between four and five o'clock, and that he remained there till after ten—some of them said after eleven o'clock."

When they were questioned about the time, none of them could remember exactly the day of the month. Some said it was after Christmas, and "some in the holy-days. They all agreed, however, that it was on a Sunday, and that it was the birthday of Mrs Brown's child."

Richard David Croucher was recalled.

Mr Colden: How many times was you at Ring's on Sunday evening of the twenty-second of December?

R D. Croucher: Three times, and the latest about three o'clock.

Mr Colden: Did you ever publish the handbills about apparitions, murder, and so forth?

R. D. Croucher: No, I never did, nor do I know who did. I was at a Mrs Wellham's, and I saw one there which I asked leave to bring it to Ring's, but I was not permitted, and that is all I know of them or ever saw of them.

This was the end of the prosecution's case. It was twenty-five minutes past two in the morning, and the examination had closed. Seventy-five witnesses had been sworn, although Coleman does not give the testimony of all of them.

Colonel Burr then read to the jury the following passages from Hale's *Pleas of the Crown*:

> In some cases presumptive evidences go far to prove a person guilty, though there be no express proof of the fact to be committed by him, but then it must be very warily pressed, for it is better five guilty persons should escape unpunished, than one innocent person should die.
>
> If a horse be stolen from A. and the same day B. be found upon him, it is a strong presumption that B. stole him, yet I do remember before a very learned and wary judge in such an instance, B. was condemned and executed at Oxford assizes, and yet within two assizes after, C. being apprehended for another robbery and convicted, upon his judgment and execution, confessed that he was the man that stole the horse, and being closely pursued desired B., a stranger, to walk his horse for him, while he turned aside upon a necessary occasion, and escaped; and B. was apprehended with the horse and died innocently.
>
> Another that happened in my remembrance in Staffordshire where A. was long missing, and upon strong presumptions B. was supposed to have murdered him, and to have consumed him to ashes, in an oven, that he should not be found, whereupon B. was indicted of murder, and convicted and executed, and within one year after A. returned, being indeed sent beyond sea by B. against his will, and so, though B. justly deserved death, yet

> he really was not guilty of the offence for which he suffered.

There is some question about exactly what happened next. Coleman says that the defense counsel proposed that the case be submitted for a verdict without further argument, but that the Assistant Attorney General wanted an adjournment similar to the one they had had the previous night. The *New York Daily Advertiser,* however, says that Colden moved for an adjournment, and that Hamilton rose and said that the case was clear; it required no "laboured elucidation;"[52] he was willing to rest on the points brought out. Coleman says that Mr Colden complained that he had not slept since the morning the trial began, so that he had been awake for forty-four hours and he was "sinking under his fatigue;" since the prisoner's counsel would probably take several hours to present their closing address to the jury, he could not begin his own closing address until morning. He really did not have the strength to go on that night, and unless the Court was willing to grant an adjournment, he would have to accept the desire of the defense to submit the case now. He wanted the adjournment because he thought it important that the jury hear his comments on the testimony.

Whatever Mr Colden wanted, the Court felt that they had heard enough. Coleman says that they said it would be "too hard to keep the jury together another night without the conveniencies necessary to repose, and they therefore did not think it proper." The Chief Justice charged the jury, making the following observations, as reported by Coleman:

> That from the manner in which the trial had been conducted, he had been led to suppose that the arguments of the counsel would have afforded him sufficient time to adjust and

arrange the mass of evidence, which, in its progress, had been brought into view—that it had, unexpectedly, became his duty to charge them immediately after the testimony was closed—but that he submitted to this with less reluctance from a persuasion that a minute detail was not essential to enable them to determine on the case according to its justice, as the evidence applying to the points on which it ought to be decided, in his opinion, lay in a small compass—That the question they had to decide involved considerations of great moment, both to the public and the prisoner—To the public as deeply interested in the detection and punishment of crimes of the atrocious nature of that with which the prisoner was charged—To the prisoner, as on their verdict depended his life and every thing dear to the human mind—That these observations were only pertinent so far as they might operate to stimulate their attention and prompt a dispassionate estimate of the evidence—but that they ought not to be permitted to influence them from pronouncing the result of their investigations according to the impressions they had made on their minds, regardless of the consequences attached to their determination—that their path of duty was clearly and distinctly traced for them *to find the prisoner guilty if in their consciences they believed him so from the evidence—to acquit him if they thought him innocent*—That previous to his considering the nature and effect of the evidence, it might be well to observe that this matter had, in a considerable degree, excited the public attention—that it had interested the passions of many, and that a variety of reports respecting it had been circulated, some of which must, unavoidably, have been communicated to them—that by whatever motive prompted, they did not deserve attention, and that they ought not to have attached to them the least consequence, or to mingle with the facts disclosed by the witnesses—that the obligation they had incurred when they became Jurors, limited them to the evidence produced on the trial, and that *that* only could justify the verdict they were called upon to give on this occasion—that in this case it was not pretended that positive proof of the commission of the murder by the prisoner was attainable, but that it had been attempted to prove his guilt by circumstantial evidence, and that if it could be established by a number of circumstances so connected as to produce a rational conviction that he was the perpetrator of the crime, it would be as much as their duty to find him guilty, as if it was made out by direct and positive testimony—that there were points in which the circumstances attempted to be combined were not so satisfactorily connected as to enable them to pronounce the prisoner guilty.—That it was doubtful whether Gulielma Sands left the house of Elias Ring in company with the prisoner so as to impose it on him to account for the manner in which he had disposed of her—that the testimony respecting the one horse sleigh, did not appear to be such as to justify a presumption, that the prisoner had personally any agency in them, for that if the relation of Susannah Broad did not satisfy them, that the sleigh was taken out of the lumber yard of the prisoner's brother at or about the time Gulielma Sands disappeared, it must be evident that the relations of the other witnesses respecting a sleigh and the cries of distress heard near the Manhattan Well could have no application to the prisoner—that *Mrs Broad's* testimony was confused as to the time, and indistinct and unsatisfactory as to circumstances—that the prisoner appeared to be a young man—that it was fully proved that he had sustained a fair character, and that he was of a mild disposition—that it was difficult to discover what inducement could have actuated him in the commission of the crime with which he was charged—that the declarations made by the prisoner after he became an object of suspicion did not appear to be inconsistent with innocence—that the witnesses produced on the part of the prisoner had accounted for the manner in which he spent the evening, excepting a few minutes—that from the account the medical gentlemen, who had been examined, had given of the state of the Corpse of Gulielma, soon after it was taken out of the Well, it was very doubtful whether she had been exposed to any other violence than that occasioned by the drowning—that intimation had been given in the course of the trial, tending to question the credibility of some of the witnesses—but that it was not necessary to examine this point, for admitting all the circumstances related by the witnesses on the

> part of the prosecution to be stated without any disposition to discolour them to the prejudice of the prisoner, the court were unanimously of opinion that the proof was insufficient to warrant a verdict against him, and that with this general charge they committed the prisoner's case to their consideration.

Coleman ended his transcript with these words:

> *The Jury then went out, and returned in about five minutes with a verdict*—NOT GUILTY.

CHAPTER SEVEN

PUBLIC REACTION

Thus ended the trial of Levi Weeks. Judge Lansing's instructions to the jury left them almost no choice but to acquit the accused. Catherine Ring and Elma's friends were outraged.

Catherine's anger was reflected in the city. A neighbor of the Rings wrote a letter saying that it was certainly justifiable to ask the public to suspend judgment on the prisoner before the verdict, but "to insinuate a suspicion that the ill-fated girl was *herself* the perpetrator, is such an outrage on probability that all who are acquainted with the circumstances must hear the remark with indignation." The writer went on to say that Elma had not had a melancholy disposition—on the contrary, she had been "uniformly cheerful and serene," especially on that Sunday. "*Her expectation of becoming a bride on the morrow was the natural cause of her liveliness.* Alas, how soon was the gay prospect blackened by shades of death! . . . Her murderer yet lives, but let him tremble with horror at the vengeance that inevitably awaits him."[53]

Bad feeling at the verdict prompted newspapers to argue for the fairness of the trial. The jury, the *Commercial Advertiser* said on April 2, 1800, was "as respectable as ever appeared in this city." The eloquence of the defense counsel had been attacked by many citizens; the

Commercial Advertiser said that the verdict had been reached because the prisoner had produced "clear and unequivocal proof . . . of his innocence" and not at all because of the machinations of the defense attorneys, and that the verdict must be "a pleasing circumstance to this young man, whose character at the trial appeared irreproachable and uncommonly amiable and to his respectable connections."

The "Gentleman of the Bar" produced a pamphlet in which he decried the rumor, apparently still current, that a New Jersey man had stepped forward and confessed himself an accessory to the murder. "This tale," he said, "was destitute of the smallest foundation." One had only to observe "the perfect artlessness" of Levi Weeks's face where "guilt could never have lurked." Throughout the trial, Levi's face "appeared the index of a virtuous and benevolent heart; his deportment that of a man incapable of the smallest approach to the crimes with which error had accused him."[54]

James Hardie called the verdict "a triumph of innocence." When Elma was first discovered to be missing, he wrote, the accusation against Levi appeared trivial, but then it began to grow, fed "either by the malicious and studied designs of his enemies, or what is more probable, by that propensity which thoughtless people generally exercise, in propagating slander."

Now, Hardie said, Levi Weeks had, "after the most lengthy and impartial trial which perhaps was ever held in New York" been found innocent by a jury of his peers. It was not surprising that this young man, "who had been universally beloved by the most respectable inhabitants of New York for his probity, industry, temperance, suavity of disposition, gentility of manners, etc., in short, for a display of all those virtues which are most ornamental in the human character, would attract a large share of the human attention."[55]

This deluge of praise from the press for the accused man, with its heavy emphasis on the "respectability" of his supporters, had apparently no effect upon the attitude of the citizenry; indeed, the similarity of tone of this praise may have roused suspicions among them. As we shall see, there was reason to believe that Ezra Weeks had not been above bribery in his zeal to protect his brother. In any case, the people of New York did not believe that justice had been served. The judge appeared to them to have been biased in favor of the defense attorneys, whose cleverness did not persuade the multitude that Elma had ventured forth on that snowy December evening to tear her own clothes and fling herself into a well, and the trial had ended with surprising abruptness. Levi Weeks was widely perceived to be a murderer whose "respectable connections" had moved heaven and earth to get him off. Elma Sands had been traduced as a trollope and a suicide, and the public was outraged. It has been said that Levi Weeks was threatened and insulted whenever he ventured forth in the streets, and that he was forced to leave the city, never to return. He lived for a time in South Deerfield, Massachusetts, but the story followed him there, and eventually he left. It is said that he spent his life moving from place to place as a kind of social leper. . .[56]

Surely awareness of the case was not lessened by the issuance of the three transcripts of the trial. Coleman's transcript had been publicly announced while the trial was in progress, by the publisher, John Furman, who said that "the anxiety of the public may be gratified in the course of a few days, by having a fair, candid and accurate account, containing every particular."[57]

The shortcomings of Coleman's report notwithstanding, it is by far the most detailed account available to us; also, it is considered important as the first attempt following the Revolution to make a verbatim report of a criminal trial. In his preface, Coleman had sharp criticism for the work of his two colleagues. That of the "Gentleman of the Bar"—David Longworth—was such a "paltry performance," he would not have descended to notice it, were it not for a particularly glaring misrepresentation: this pamphlet was "trumpeted around the streets" as the *whole* trial of Levi Weeks. Not so, said Coleman. Longworth's was an inaccurate, slipshod report, hardly complete, and he hoped its author would not be encouraged by its large sale to produce similar deceptions.

William Coleman was even less flattering to James Hardie, although he made his remarks "with some reluctance" because of Hardie's excellent reputation. Some of the testimony Hardie attributed to witnesses was erroneous, Coleman wrote. Hardie had reported that Joseph Watkins had testified to hearing two distinct voices through the partition—Elias Ring's and Elma's. Coleman's verbatim account held that Watkins *thought* one of the voices was Elias Ring's, but he could not identify even the sex of the other speaker. Hardie had admitted that he could not provide a verbatim account because he did not know shorthand, but he had cavalierly dismissed much of the testimony as not being worth reading, since it "appeared to have no connection with the point in question." Coleman acknowledged that Hardie's errors may have resulted partly from his inconvenient position in the courtroom, and his intentions may have been "innocent," but "surely a conscientious man cannot but feel some degree of uneasiness, that he has done a thing in the face of the public—at once so injurious to truth and to the individual who is affected by it." That was, of course, Elias Ring.

Poor Elma was beyond caring, although Catherine Ring was certainly not.

Coleman pointed out that it was because he alone had taken great pains to be sure that his transcript was "minutely accurate and strictly impartial" that the publication of it had been delayed, allowing the two other reports to appear first. He ended his preface with the comment that he would make no remark upon the guilt or innocence of Levi Weeks. The court had delivered a verdict of innocent, and the matter was concluded.

This seemingly innocuous statement upset Ezra Weeks. He offered Coleman $500 to alter the note or omit it altogether. This attempt at bribery raises serious questions about the outpourings of praise for Levi and the verdict from the press and the other two trial reporters. And it raises serious questions about James Hardie's "innocent intentions" in publishing a version of Joseph Watkins' testimony that served the purposes of the defense. Needless to say, the fact that Ezra Weeks was prepared to spend a considerable sum of money to buy support for his brother—or at least to suppress even the mildest suggestion of doubt about the verdict—calls into question the motivation of Joseph Watkins and his family for their shocking testimony, much of which was strongly contradicted by Catherine Ring and others who knew Elma and the Rings.

Coleman refused to accept Ezra Weeks's money. Ezra then offered to buy out the entire edition of Coleman's transcript for $1,500. Coleman refused this offer as well, saying that he could not be bought for all the money in New York City. The story goes that Ezra Weeks was impressed by Coleman's incorruptibility and that he and Coleman became friends.[58]

CHAPTER EIGHT

HISTORIC PERSPECTIVE

For the next hundred years writers were not apt to dismiss the case of Levi Weeks lightly. All attempts made immediately after the trial to stifle the controversy were fruitless. In 1861, more than half a century later, a record was published, which appears in the *Manuals of the Corporation of the City of New York,* reporting eerie sights and sounds at the Manhattan Well: shrieks, flashes of fire in the sky, and the appearance of a figure draped in white. When unbelievers were present, the record says, these phenomena did not occur. Included in the *Manuals* is a letter from the Reverend Doctor Ferris, Chancellor of New York University, in which he writes that his aged aunt had known Elma well, and had always spoken of her as "the most lovely creature she ever saw;" this aunt, according to Doctor Ferris, had seen Elma on the "evening of her fatal sleigh-ride, when she was just ready to step into the sleigh"[59]—a piece of information which apparently was denied to the unfortunate Cadwallader Colden.

The influence of Doctor Ferris' aged aunt was still felt nearly eighty years later in a letter which appeared in the *New York Sun* for June 8, 1937, under the heading "A Crime of 1799":

On a bright, moonlight Sunday night in the winter of 1799, when the streets of New York were deep with snow, one of the popular young men of the period, Levi Weeks, drove up to the residence of his sweetheart, Miss Gulielma Sands, to invite the young lady for a sleigh ride. Miss Sands lived with her aunt and uncle on the then fashionable thorofare of Greenwich Street. The aunt accompanied the young couple to the door, bid them not to stay out too late, and closed the door before they had reached the waiting sleigh. It was the last time she saw her niece alive.

Weeks was accused. He vehemently declared his innocence, asserting that just before entering the sleigh on the evening in question, the two had quarreled over some trivial matter, and that he had driven off, leaving Miss Sands at the gateway of her home. The case became the cause célèbre of the day.

Weeks escaped conviction through the testimony of the aunt who testified that although she saw the couple leave the front door, she did not see them enter the sleigh. There is also the tradition that either Hamilton or Burr greatly influenced the jury by a tricky arrangement of candles which illuminated the prosecution's principal witness in a ghastly manner.

Years afterward when Spring Street became a place of homes, each with a little garden, the once-celebrated murder mystery was again brought to public notice by one of the dwellers on the street. In digging for his garden, the occupant at 116 Spring Street uncovered the ancient well. It was 80 feet deep, partly filled

> with earth. Old-timers took great pleasure in telling the new generation of the sad story of pretty, young Gulielma Sands.

Also included in the *Manuals* is a sketch of the Ring boardinghouse, which was pulled down in the middle of the century. It is a three-story structure with attic windows and a peaked roof, set in a ragged row of wooden buildings. A slatted shed, held up by three poles, juts out from the first story and extends over the doorway and the sidewalk. A man and a woman, dressed like Quakers, are crossing the cobblestoned street. On the corner of the street, next to the low curb, is a long-handled pump where Catherine Lyon tended the woman who had fallen. It was there that Lyon said she saw the shape of Elma, and spoke to her, less than half an hour before she heard cries of murder coming from the Well.

The murder of Elma Sands inspired at least two novels in the nineteenth century. One, *Norman Leslie* (1835) by Theodore S. Fay, is a two-volume melodramatic hodgepodge, set in New York and several European capitals. The villain is a European aristocrat. Norman Leslie, based on Levi Weeks, is in fact innocent, but he is the victim of a nefarious plot, hatched for purposes of greed. A case of mistaken identity is involved: a woman's body is found in the East River, but it is not the body of the woman Leslie is accused of murdering. The second novel, *Guilty or Not Guilty: The True Story of the Manhattan Well* (1870), stays closer to actual events. It presents life as idyllic in the Ring household, where Elma and Hope live while they go to school. Elma, who has a saintly disposition, falls deeply in love with the boarder Levi, who is very handsome, but whose face darkens at moments with an ominous expression of great cruelty. Levi is ruled by two passions: "pride and love of money." His wealthy brother Ezra knows about the romance but he knows too that Elma is a penniless orphan without impressive connections and so he is opposed to the match. He urges Levi to free Elma to wed another, but Levi says, "No; I *could* not and *would* not do that; I would sooner put her out of the way than see another enjoy her." And put her out of the way he does.

The book is unsigned, but the dedication and information supplied by Janet Dempsey, town historian at Cornwall, New York, identify the author as Keturah Connah, David Ring's daughter and Catherine Ring's granddaughter:

> To thee, my venerated GRANDMOTHER, I dedicate this, my feeble attempt at authorship. The truths which it contains I gathered in childhood from thy own lips, and though thou has been resting for many a year, and thy name and age stand registered upon imperishable marble, I see thee vividly as in years gone by, when thou didst sit, the center of an admiring throng, and tell to us the sad history of Cousin Elma.[60]

Another retelling of the murder is found in a clipping from an unidentified newspaper which was pasted inside a copy of Coleman's report in the library of the New-York Historical Society. The clipping is undated but the reference to *Norman Leslie* would place it some time after 1835. The article is entitled "The Murder of Elma Sands":

> Among the reminiscences of the Fifth Ward there is none of more exciting interest than that of the murder of Gulielma Sands . . .

Theodore S. Fay found the materials for his romance of *Norman Leslie* in the sad fate of this unfortunate girl. . . .

Gulielma, or, as she was most generally called, Elma Sands, was residing with a Quaker family, relatives of her mother, by the name of Ring who were keeping a boardinghouse in Greenwich street. In the month of June, 1799, a young man of respectable connections, named Levi Weeks, made application for board and was received as an inmate in the house. He here became enamoured of Miss Sands, and paid her, for months, the most assiduous attentions, and they were generally looked upon by the rest of the boarders, as well as by the relatives of Miss Sands, as affianced lovers. During the month of December of the same year, she disclosed to Hope Sands, a sister of Mrs Ring, that she was engaged to be married to Weeks, but declared that she must not reveal it, as it was the earnest desire of Weeks to keep it a secret for a short time. On the evening of the 22nd of December, she revealed the same fact to Mrs Ring, and said that eight o'clock was the hour appointed for the consummation of the ceremony, and at that time Weeks was to call for her. Mrs Ring assisted her in dressing for the occasion, and borrowed a muff, from a neighbor, for her use.

At eight o'clock, Weeks came in, and took his seat in the common sitting-room, appropriated to the boarders, but, shortly after, as a step was heard descending the stairs, took up his hat and left. In the entry, or passage-way, two voices were heard whispering for about a minute, when the front door opened, and was immediately closed. . . .

From that moment Elma Sands was not seen alive. . . .

Days passed, and nothing was heard of the missing girl, until the borrowed muff was found near Manhattan Well, by a boy about thirteen years of age. . . . This led to further examination. . . . The result was the discovery of the body of the murdered girl. . . .

From the testimony brought forward on the trial, it is quite evident that the unfortunate victim of seduction and murder (for it was distinctly proven against Weeks that he had won her affections, and that her virtue fell a sacrifice to his arts), was enticed from her home and conveyed in a sleigh to the Well, and there, in the stillness of the holy Sabbath, brutally murdered. Her cries for help were heard but unheeded, and the murderer passed from the desecrated spot to mingle among his kind, with a feeling of joy at the thought that his foul deed had escaped the eye of mortal scrutiny.

Suspicion at once rested upon Levi Weeks. He was arrested and his trial commenced on the 31st of March ensuing. . . .

The circumstantial evidence against the prisoner was most conclusive, but, through the ingenuity of his counsel, he was acquitted. The public voice, however, failed to endorse the verdict of the jury, and when he appeared in the streets, he was followed by shouts of derision and execration, which, proving at last too much for his powers of endurance, or

> dreading the execution of some act of public vengeance that might prove fatal, he fled the city, never to return.

It is obvious from the tenor of this article that the general perception was that Elma had been having an affair with Levi, who had promised to marry her, and that he had murdered her to avoid keeping his promise. The same perception appears in a much longer and more detailed article in *Harper's New Monthly* for spring, 1872, by Edward S. Gould. In this article, entitled "The Manhattan Well Mystery: (December 22, 1799)," Gould tells the story which is now so familiar to us, with some emphasis on the evidence against Weeks: "It appeared by the testimony that Weekes [sic] was *very* intimate with Gulielma . . . and Elma had confidentially informed Mrs Ring and Hope Sands that she and Weekes were to be privately married." The Well, he says, "now stands in the rear of a carpenter's shop at the end of an alley, No. 89½ Greene Street, a hundred feet or more north of Spring Street." He adds, "The distance from Ring's house to the Well was about half a mile."

Gould then summarizes the cases for the prosecution and for the defense, although in a way that is by no means evenhanded. He says, for instance, parenthetically, that "the prosecution had proved that a track of a one-horse sleigh was found in the snow very near the Well, and quite off from the road." In his discussion of the case for the defense, he uses italics to emphasize his point: ". . . several doctors gave opinions as to what, other than strangulation by hand, *might* have caused the marks about the neck. They intimated that the marks on the body *might* have arisen from remaining several days in the water and then being brought into contact with the cold air of winter. One of the physicians made a post-mortem examination and proved the deceased was *not* 'likely to become a mother.' " Although he encloses the latter phrase in quotation marks, Gould is not in fact quoting from the transcript of the trial: in that transcript the doctor says forthrightly that Elma "was not pregnant." This is an amusing illustration of the differences in attitude toward sexual matters of the eighteenth and nineteenth centuries. It is perhaps pertinent to note here that Levi and Elma were granted considerable privacy in the Ring household because it was believed that they were going to be married. Those were pre-Victorian days.

After summarizing what he considers the main points of the trial, Gould says, "And finally the counsel on both sides took the very unusual course—unusual, that is, in a trial for murder—of submitting the case without argument to the jury, under charge of the judge." It is the judge's charge with which Gould takes issue, and his comments are worth reprinting in their entirety:

> The charge of Chief Justice Lansing was the most extraordinary part of the trial. After saying that he was taken by surprise in being called on to charge the jury before he had the usual opportunity of preparing a digest of the testimony for the jury's consideration, and after some incidental comments, he proceeded to remark, quietly and as a matter of course, that it was *very doubtful* whether the deceased left the house of Elias Ring on that Sunday evening in company with the prisoner; that the witnesses on the part of the prisoner had accounted for the manner in which he spent the evening, 'excepting in a few minutes;' that, from the testimony of the physicians, it was very doubtful whether the deceased had been

exposed to any violence other than that occasioned by the drowning; that it was difficult to discover what motive could have actuated the prisoner in the commission of such a crime; and that *the Court was unanimously of opinion that the proof was insufficient to warrant a verdict against the prisoner!*

The jury retired, but they returned in five minutes with a verdict of *not guilty*.

Perhaps, in a state of weariness and exhaustion—though *that* had really nothing to do with the merits of the case—the jury, under such a charge, might plead that they had no discretion left, and were compelled to render such a verdict. Perhaps they wished 'the thing over,' and caught at a pretext for simplifying their duty. If that were so, they seem to have lost sight of their *rights* in the premises. Or they may have felt themselves justified in evading what the Chief Justice was so ready to assume—the entire responsibility of deciding on the facts.

The Chief Justice, in his charge, voluntarily took upon himself the jury's exclusive prerogative. The question of fact, whether Levi and Elma went out together, was a question for the jury alone to decide, and it was a vital point; for if they *did* go out together, it was incumbent on Levi to account for her; and if he could not account for her, his case was gone. The testimony undoubtedly fell short of positive proof. The testimony was circumstantial, and the proof only inferential; but that is precisely the state of things that calls for the free deliberation and action of a jury, *not* under instructions from the Court. To *caution* a jury on a doubtful point, and to tell them that they are bound to give the prisoner the benefit of a reasonable doubt, is proper and customary; but to *instruct* them on the doubt is another thing.

Again the reference to the prisoner's *motive* was gratuitous. That was a point for the prisoner's counsel to make; and if he had made it, the opposite counsel would have replied, 'We are not bound to prove a motive. We have proved a murder, and we have brought it to the prisoner's door. Shift it away from that door, if you can. Convince the jury, if you can, that it does not lie there. You can not contrive even a theory of the death of this woman, other than her murder by Weekes, unless you set up suicide. And what was the motive for *that*? If a motive for homicide is indispensable, a motive for suicide is indispensable. Besides, does a woman select drowning herself in a well as a method of suicide? And does she take off her hat and shawl, and handkerchief around her neck, and tear open the bosom of her dress, and take off her shoes, *and all the while keep hold of her muff,* and then jump into the Well head-foremost? *We* say that the woman was strangled by the hands of her murderer near the Well, that the dress was torn in the struggle, and that the muff, shawl, and handkerchief were thrown into the Well after the woman.'

As to the *alibi,* the judge virtually instructed the jury that they were to accept the statement of time given by the Weekeses and

> their visitor without question or investigation; and he made the time shorter than the witnesses did—"a few minutes."
>
> The testimony of the physicians for the prosecution was affirmative and positive as to the infliction of violence on the body before it was thrown into the Well. The physicians for the defense did not go beyond saying that the marks *might have been* produced by exposure to the air after a long immersion in the water. The judge told the jury that it was very doubtful whether the physicians for the prosecution were right about it!
>
> The concluding sentence of the charge is the most remarkable of all. A mass of testimony which had occupied the court for nearly three days, and which the judge admitted that he had not time to digest as he intended to do, was, nevertheless, disposed of in two lines—the Court was unanimously of opinion that the proof was insufficient to warrant a verdict against the prisoner!
>
> The popular version of the result of the trial was that Weekes was acquitted by the Jury; the true version is that he was acquitted by the Court.
>
> As all the parties to this trial have passed to their account, it is safe to say that the mystery of the Manhattan Well Murder must remain forever *legally* unsolved.

Mr Gould went on to discuss the stories about Croucher and the candelabra or candles and concluded that they were "in every way immaterial and unimportant. The result of the trial was entirely independent of 'the candle;'

and one might venture to say that it was hardly 'worth the candle.' . . . The crime itself was a terrible tragedy. The trial was almost a farce."[61]

This strong feeling about the unfairness of the verdict faded in the mid-twentieth century, when discussions of the trial appeared almost without exception in books about Alexander Hamilton and Aaron Burr. Certainly the transcript of the Levi Weeks trial offers rare insight into actions of Burr and Hamilton in the courtroom. The biographers of these men tend to believe that the prosecution case was weak, and that the verdict was the only possible one under the circumstances. Or at least that is the way in which they present the affair to their readers.

Milton Lomask, in his biography of Burr, draws at least one conclusion which does not appear to be borne out by the transcript of the trial. On the Sunday night in question, he says, "young Weeks was seen holding Elma's coat for her as she prepared to leave the . . . boardinghouse. None of the observers of the scene were certain that Weeks departed with her, although some of them assumed as much. Testimony offered at a later point indicated that he did leave the house for a time, but not with Gulielma."[62] Catherine Ring was certain that Levi left the house with Elma; this was of course an assumption on her part. But testimony did more than "indicate" that he left the house for a time; the defense used his visit to his brother's house as an alibi. No one was able to "indicate" that Levi did not leave with Elma.

Since Lomask dwells on Burr's actions for the defense, and since he paraphrases Burr's opening address to the jury, Lomask's summary of the case gives the strong impression that Elma was a girl of easy virtue and melancholy disposition who had probably killed herself.

In his biography of Alexander Hamilton, Broadus Mitchell dismisses Colden's case more airily. Levi and

Elma, he says, were "fellow lodgers" at the boardinghouse, and, "about eight o'clock on the evening of December 22, 1799, Gulielma went out on an unexplained errand." Moving along from that odd description, he says, after mentioning the finding of the body: "Excitement was busily fed by unsupported accusations made by acquaintances of Gulielma—and by rumor—not to speak of the exhibit of the body to public gaze on the street." Weeks was indicted because of "popular clamor":

> Colden had only circumstantial evidence to present, and that exceedingly thin . . . The defense offered a score of witnesses who testified to young Weeks's excellent character. Gulielma was variously described as of a cheerful or melancholy disposition, lively or prone to threats of suicide, given to mysterious night outings, and fond of laudanum. Complaints by today's New Yorkers against thin partitions between apartments are nothing new: the party wall between the lodging-house* and the dwelling next door was made of boards, lathed and plastered on each side. The court allowed testimony of the estimable neighbor: he said that he had been disturbed by the creaking of the bed on the other side of the partition, in which, it was implied, Gulielma and a male companion—not Weeks—were furiously making love.[63]

One biographer of Hamilton goes so far as to suggest that the murderer was Catherine Ring, "a betrayed wife jilted by her former paramour for the same younger and

*The Ring house was actually a boardinghouse because meals were served there.

more beautiful woman who had also captured her husband." Her "well motivated, lying accomplice" was Richard Croucher.[64] Biographers of the defense attorneys have written Elma off as "none too virtuous,"[65] and "promiscuous with her numerous suitors;"[66] she has even been called a prostitute.[67] None of these writers shows interest in who, if Levi was innocent, really killed Elma Sands. In a way one could say that here the victim is found guilty.

A more sober discussion is provided by Julius Goebel in his history of Hamilton's law practice. He notes that the trial differed from modern trials at the outset in that witnesses were encouraged by both prosecution and defense to give free-flowing accounts rather than to respond only to questions, while at the same time interruption of testimony by opposing counsel "was tolerated to a remarkable degree." Goebel likens the trial to "an inquest designed to establish the truth" rather than "a prosecution and defense of a murder charge." In addition, hearsay evidence was admitted that would not be admitted today. In 1800 there were few precedents for hearsay rulings; the 1787 *Pleas of the Crown* by Hawkins was the Bible of New York lawyers at that time, and most of Hawkins' precedents come from *State Trials,* which contains accounts of trials written by laymen whose primary purpose was the entertainment of the public.[68]

Goebel points out that both the prosecution and the defense were on the same level, so to speak, because Mr Colden had no strong law-enforcement mechanism behind him, and indeed, Colden's task was made more difficult by the notoriety the case received before the trial: "There were assuredly busybodies who were anxious to share the limelight. The old woman, Susanna Broad, is an obvious example, and so it would seem were Catherine Lyon and the Van Nordens."[69] Goebel does not mention Henry Orr, another witness who said he heard cries coming from the direction of the Manhattan Well, but he would undoubtedly dismiss his testimony along with Catherine Lyon's.

Goebel dismisses also what he calls "the story about the sleigh and its occupants which was so clumsily built up that it wanted all probative force and collapsed under attack."[69] This statement is not borne out by the trial transcript. There were, of course, several stories about the sleigh. Willam and Ann Lewis said that on the Monday morning after Elma's disappearance they saw sleigh tracks going to the Well. Andrew Blanck, the father of the boy who found the muff, also testified that he saw sleigh tracks around the Well. Buthrong Anderson, Joseph Stringham and Joseph Cornwell all testified that they saw a sleigh with "two or three people" in it, going at a full gallop. Margaret Freeman said she saw a one-horse sleigh with two men and a woman in it pass her as she walked in the street. It is not apparent from Coleman's transcript that any of this testimony collapsed under attack. It is interesting that although only one person was accused of murdering Elma some of these witnesses said they saw *three* people in the sleigh.

Goebel goes on to fault Colden for not discovering before the trial that the young boys who found the muff were illiterate and did not know what an oath signified. The boys were consequently rejected as incompetent by the Court. This event appeared, Goebel says, to damage Colden's credibility. Goebel criticizes Colden also for bringing out "little or none" of "the facts surrounding the alleged engagement of the deceased and Weeks."[69] Goebel does not note at the same time, however, that the defense objected to Catherine Ring's testimony about Elma's confidences, and the judge upheld the objection.

Goebel believes that Colden's "most egregious error" lay in "the quality of the medical testimony," which he considers crucial; the evidence of the men who lifted the body from the Well was "equivocal,"[69] by which he means it is open to various interpretations.

Instead of using the testimony of the physicians who had been called to the coroner's inquest, Colden used the testimony of doctors who had not seen the body until several days after it had been recovered from the Well. The former doctors testified for the defense, whom Goebel congratulates for securing their "most telling evidence" that there were no marks of violence upon the body. Since Colden's contention was that Elma had been murdered, the testimony of these doctors would have been useless to him. Goebel goes on to say, "Since the whole city knew that the cadaver had been opened to discover if the girl were pregnant, the inference was obvious that the marks seen after the event by the beholders were the result of the autopsy."[70]

The whole city may have known this, but the whole city was apparently not convinced that there had been no marks of violence on the body before the inquest, because Levi Weeks was forced to leave New York after the trial by hostile public opinion. Apart from this, the testimony of the physicians who had attended the inquest does not jibe with the actions of the coroner's jury which had brought in a verdict of willful murder. Goebel makes no attempt to reconcile these inconsistencies.

Finally, Goebel says, "the testimony about intimacies between Gulielma and Weeks was blunted by testimony tending to show that similar intimacies between the girl and Ring . . . might have occurred in the absence of the wife."[71] The Assistant Attorney General, Goebel comments, was discomfited by the Watkins' testimony. Unquestionably he was discomfited; but Goebel does not mention the numerous inconsistencies which Colden managed to elicit from Watkins on cross-examination. It is true that the prosecutor did not take advantage of these inconsistencies by developing them to any extent. He was obviously rattled. And he had, of course, the burden of the entire prosecution while the defense attorneys could spell each other. He had also the burden of contesting three famous lawyers.

Commenting on the medical testimony, Dr George D. Lundberg, a modern pathologist and the editor and vice-president for scientific information for the *Journal of the American Medical Association,* writes that, after closely reviewing the account of the trial, "we are left with obscure conclusions and certainly not enough to base a murder conviction upon, unless there were eye witnesses, other physical evidence, or similarly strong findings."

He is inclined to believe, however, that "Elma was a victim of homicide rather than accident or suicide, based upon markings on her neck that were rather consistently described." Dr Lundberg says that "the amount of dissection that was performed is quite obscure" and that "the findings as described [are] virtually indecipherable." It is unclear how much clothing was removed during the various examinations, he says, and the problem is further complicated by the fact that postmortem decomposition can mimic antemortem wounds. "The problem of immersion in water also causes confusion," Lunderg writes, "both of fluid within the body, (and it is unclear where, anatomically, this occurred) and skin changes, including coloration."[72]

Robert Bard, professor of law at the University of Connecticut, writes that "under the rules of procedure pertaining to New York criminal trials in 1800, which in relevant part are substantially identical to those controlling a modern criminal trial, Levi Weeks was almost certain to be acquitted."

Today, however, there would probably be evidence that

clearly established Weeks's guilt or innocence. A significant source of additional evidence would be Weeks's own testimony. But the right of a defendant to testify in his own defense was only established in New York in 1877. Whether or not Weeks would have elected to testify would depend on a variety of factors, including his lawyers' judgment of Weeks's effectiveness as a witness.

According to Bard, Weeks had to be acquitted because the prosecution could produce neither direct nor circumstantial evidence establishing Weeks's guilt beyond reasonable doubt. There were neither eye witnesses nor physical evidence linking Weeks to the crime; no motive was established, and neither the cause nor the place of death was determined. The indictment stated two inconsistent causes of death: death by drowning and death by fatal assault. In addition, Weeks established a powerful alibi which the prosecution chose not to challenge.

The only damning circumstantial evidence against Weeks was Catherine Ring's statement that Elma had said she was to marry Weeks on the night she disappeared. But Elma's statements to Mrs Ring were, and would be today, inadmissable as hearsay, as Goebel has pointed out. Only the person who made the statements can testify to them. The best the prosecution could do was to attempt to prove that Weeks and Elma were lovers. According to Bard, today, the defense would have vigorously objected to the prosecution's attempts to prove this, saying that the testimony had no relevance to possible motive.

Bard finds it unlikely that Weeks would even have been indicted today based on the available evidence. Probably, because of the advances in forensic medicine, evidence would be found that could clarify the circumstances of Elma's death and possibly even identify her murderer. And today, Weeks would face an efficient police force and a far more formidable prosecutor. "Because Weeks could enlist the services of such legal stars as Hamilton, Burr and Livingston, he was able to successfully demonstrate the *legal* weaknesses of the prosecution's case . . . and win acquittal. But he was unable to prove his innocence to the public, the police or to the prosecutor," Bard asserts.[73]

In 1957 Meyer Berger wrote an article for the *New York Times* about Elma's murder. He made a pilgrimage by taxi to the supposed site of the Manhattan Well:

> A few doors up from Spring Street on the west side of Greene you come upon an untidy factory alley. Winds stir sooty papers in it and high walls hem it in. In twilight it has a sinister, brooding air.
>
> Down under the alley flagstone lies a deep well, part of the water system used at the end of the eighteenth century. It was out in the country then, on the edge of the Lispenard Meadows. It figured in an unsolved mystery a month after George Washington died. . .
>
> This was the first of New York's so-called "love murders." And the other night, a little after dark, a reporter looked for the old well cover in the alley at 89 Greene Street, using tapers made of sooty papers he found there.
>
> The cab driver who had brought the reporter to that lonely spot wondered what it was that brought him to the alley. The reporter said, "Just checking on a murder; a girl was killed here." The cabby said, "I think I read about it a coupla days ago."[74]

CHAPTER NINE

AFTERMATH

Legend has it that, in the courtroom, upon Levi's acquittal, Catherine Ring pointed at Alexander Hamilton, and cried out, "If thee dies a natural death, I shall think there is no justice in heaven!"[75]

Since, as everyone knows, Alexander Hamilton died four years later from a bullet fired by Aaron Burr, it would seem that Catherine's curse—if that was what it was—was carried out. Although Burr himself died a natural death at the ripe age of eighty, his career was destroyed by Hamilton's death.

The lives of the defense lawyers were stained by violence: two years before the tragic encounter at Weehawken, Hamilton's nineteen-year-old son Philip was killed in a duel. Brockholst Livingston killed a man named James Jones in a duel, an event which "produced great excitement at the time" and which was said to have left Livingston under a cloud of "gloom from which he never recovered."[76] This death did not, apparently, affect Livingston's career. He became a justice of the New York supreme court and in 1807 was appointed by Jefferson to the U.S. Supreme Court. In addition the cloud of gloom hanging over him was not always noticeable: Justice Joseph

Storey found him to be an "accessible and easy" man, who enjoyed "with great good humor, the vivacities of the wit and the moralist."[77] Livingston served as first vice-president of the New-York Historical Society and assisted in the incorporation of the New York public school system.

Although he had fought at least one duel himself, Livingston prevented William Coleman, who had denounced duelling as a "horrid custom" in the *Evening Post,* from fighting a duel with a newspaper rival by having both men arrested. The aftermath of this was another duel: the Collector of the Port of New York said publicly that Coleman had secretly arranged the arrest, out of cowardice. Coleman challenged the Collector, a man named Thompson, and they met in a blinding snowstorm at the foot of Twenty-Third Street, then the outskirts of the city. Thompson was mortally wounded on the third round, achieving the dubious distinction of being the last man to die in a duel in the state of New York. Coleman's career was not damaged.

In 1813 Aaron Burr's beloved daughter Theodosia took passage on a ship from Charleston, where she lived with her husband, to New York to meet her father. The ship vanished and Theodosia was never heard from again. It is possible that the ship was seized by pirates. Theodosia was thirty years old.

An equally bizarre fate awaited Judge Lansing. On December 12, 1829, he went to New York on a business trip and checked into the City Hotel. He had dinner and went to his room. He had an engagement to take tea with Robert Raye at six o'clock that evening. At about five o'clock he left his room, presumably to put a letter on board the steamboat to Albany and then to meet Mr Raye. He was never seen again. He disappeared completely and mysteriously. His family advertised for him in the newspaper:

Judge Lansing was a healthy man of seventy-six who had never been known to suffer mental lapses. When last seen he was dressed in black and had powdered hair. It was requested that anyone who had knowledge of him should report to the City Hotel. No one responded.[78] Evidence that the judge was murdered was said to have been given to noted journalist and politician Thurlow Weed years after Lansing's disappearance, but Weed decided against revealing it. He hinted that acquisition of property had prompted the crime, and that the heirs of the murderer were wealthy because of it. However, the murderer was long dead, Weed said just before his own death, and descendants of the murderer now held positions of public trust. He did not wish to injure their reputations. Thurlow Weed died in 1882, and the incidents leading to Lansing's death and the identity of his murderer died with him.[79]

A violent end also awaited Richard David Croucher. On July 8, 1800, he was tried for rape at the Court of Oyer and Terminer. The victim was a thirteen-year-old servant girl whose mistress, a Mrs Stackhaver, had sent her to the Ring house on April 23 to scrub out Croucher's room because he was expecting "a lady and gentleman to come and see some linens that he had." She was to sleep that night with the Ring servants and clean Croucher's room the next day. But, she said, Croucher took her directly to his room when she arrived, locked the door and raped her. She told no one in the house what had happened; she said Croucher had frightened her with stories about the murdered girl in the Well. It was Mrs Stackhaver who reported the rape to the authorities; by a weird twist, Croucher had married Mrs Stackhaver the Sunday before the opening of the Weeks trial. It was obviously not a marriage made in heaven, and Brockholst Livingston, who was one of two lawyers for the defense—Cadwallader Colden was once again the prosecutor—suggested that

Mrs Stackhaver might have made up the accusation as "a short way of getting rid of a disagreeable husband." After very little deliberation, the jury found Croucher guilty, and he was sentenced to life imprisonment.[80] John Church Hamilton has noted that Croucher was subsequently pardoned; he next turned up in Virginia, where he was convicted of fraud. Eventually, Hamilton says, he returned to England where he was executed for committing "a heinous crime."[81]

Fate was somewhat kinder to the Ring family. Catherine and Elias eventually had ten children. In 1823, Elias, who apparently drank, died of yellow fever in Mobile, Alabama. After his death Catherine moved back to her childhood home in Cornwall, New York, where her mother was still living. Some years after that she turned the house into a summer boardinghouse, calling it Rose Cottage. At one time as many as fifty-six people lived there. In her old age she gathered her father's papers together and sent them to friends in England to be published. The *Journal of the Life and Gospel Labours of David Sands with Extracts from the Correspondence* was published in 1848. The book contained a note that slave labor had not been used to produce its cloth cover.

Catherine lived at Rose Cottage until her death in 1855, at the age of eighty-three. The house, now called the Old Homestead, still stands.

Hope, too, returned to Cornwall. She married George Newbold, an inventor of a plow and something of a prophet: he predicted that "man would travel through the air and under water."[82] Hope too had several children and she too lived to a ripe age. Both Hope and Catherine were considered good Samaritans by the people of Cornwall; they often charitably nursed the sick. Hope's house, like Catherine's, still stands.

There is no mention of the Weeks trial in the records

of the Society of Friends. The allegations of the Watkins family were ignored by the Quakers, who set high moral standards for themselves, and often disowned members for relatively minor transgressions. Elias Ring remained a member of the Society for sixteen years after the trial. However, he was disowned on April 3, 1816, "for the continued intemperate use of intoxicating spirits;" he had been "tenderly labored with for a considerable time . . . without producing the desired effect."[83]

Of Gulielma Sands, only one note appears in the records of the Society of Friends: she was buried in the Houston Street cemetery on January 6, 1800.[84]

AFTERWORD

Just before *The Trial of Levi Weeks* was to go to press, an editor at Academy Chicago Publishers uncovered some information about the fate of Levi Weeks.

As we have noted above, it was commonly thought that Levi Weeks fled the city in disgrace after the trial and wandered like Cain for the rest of his days.

In actual fact, a treasure trove of information about Levi Weeks's life exists in Natchez, Mississippi, where he ended his days as a respected architect and family man.

According to Natchez historians, Levi Hinckley Weeks was born in Greenwich, Massachusetts, on October 22, 1776, the eighth child of Captain Thomas Weeks and Mercy Hinckley Weeks. Captain Weeks was a teacher, surveyor and cabinetmaker; he had served as a lieutenant in the American army during the Revolutionary War and in 1780 had been a delegate to the state convention which wrote the Massachusetts constitution.[1]

Levi went to New York originally in 1798; he is mentioned for the first time in a city directory in 1800, listed as a carpenter at his brother Ezra's address in Greenwich Street.[2] Ezra is first listed in 1795.[3] In 1801, Levi is listed as an architect; in 1802 he and Ezra are listed as residing at a Harrison Street address which Ezra maintained until 1835. In 1803, probably as a result of the trial, Levi moved to South Deerfield, Massachusetts,[4] a town not far from Goshen, where he grew up and where his parents still lived.

In South Deerfield, Levi went into business with a man named Thomas Porter, selling dry goods and liquor, and apparently also doing carpentry and possibly designing some buildings.[5] In 1805 the business was terminated and Levi probably left the state.[6] In January, 1808, his father wrote to him in Cincinnati, Ohio, giving him family news and commenting that the dire effects of the Embargo—bankruptcies and unemployment—are due to "the effect of Deism"; want of "that religion in Christ Jesus" will, he says, lead to "mobs and revolution". Thomas' religious feelings were obviously a consuming passion with him, and one that was not shared by his son. In a postscript, Thomas writes: "Dear Son, I wish I knew whether any topics on religion are agreeable to you. . ."[7]

Levi spent time not only in Cincinnati but in Marietta, Ohio, and Lexington, Kentucky, before he settled in Natchez, apparently in 1809.[8] Natchez was a booming city with a reputation for attracting rogues and drifters. It was the farthest civilized city in the Republic, which made it an ideal place for a man with a social stigma. Aaron Burr may have recommended it as a suitable home for Levi; he visited Natchez in 1807 and it is more than probable that Levi's involvement with Aaron Burr had not ended after the trial. In 1812, in a chatty, affectionate letter, Ezra Weeks mentions to Levi that "Colonel Burr has been here [New York] and is at his old profession of the law."[9]

In Natchez, Levi set up as an architect, cabinetmaker and probably a builder too, in partnership with Joseph Bryant.[10] He designed several buildings—the most famous, and the only residence which can be definitely identified as his, is Auburn, an imposing Greek Revival

Auburn, built in 1812 by Levi Weeks in Natchez, Mississippi.

The most striking architectural feature in Auburn: the free-standing spiral staircase. Photograph courtesy of David Gleason, copyright © 1986 David King Gleason, from *The Great Houses of Natchez*, University Press of Mississippi.

mansion built in 1812 for Lyman Harding, a transplanted New Englander.

Of Auburn, an architectural historian has written: "The house marked a turning point in the development of architecture in the Natchez region. Its grand scale and academically derived details became the models for Natchez plantation houses built before the Civil War."[11] Levi himself called the house "the most magnificent building in the territory." The site, he said, "is one of those peculiar situations which combines all the delights of romance—the pleasures of rurality and the approach of sublimity."[12] A visitor to Auburn in 1820 said it was "the handsomest house about Natchez. . . a perfect castle."[13] Levi used many British pattern books in the design of Auburn, but his unique combination of details has given it a permanent place in the history of American architecture. Auburn still stands and has been designated a National Historic Landmark.

Several other Natchez buildings were designed by Levi Weeks, but have since been demolished. They include the Market House, City Hall, the First Bank of the State of Mississippi and the Presbyterian Church. Other residential buildings—the Briars, Monmouth, the Burling House and Glouster—are attributed to Weeks. All but Burling House are still standing. There is evidence that, besides his architectural pursuits, Levi was a cotton commission merchant, the official keeper of weights and measures and a boat-landing inspector.

In January of 1813, Levi married Ann Greenleaf, a girl of seventeen. They had four children: Thomas Greenleaf, Caroline, Levi and Sarah Catherine, the youngest, born in June of 1817.[14] Levi died prematurely in 1819 at the age of forty-three.[15] Since there was a severe yellow fever epidemic in Natchez that year, it has been assumed that he died of that disease; but a letter written on May 24,

1817, to the trustees of Jefferson College, in which Levi apologizes for not being able to keep an appointment in Washington because of his poor health, has given rise to the belief that he died from a long, debilitating illness.[16] Levi's burial place is not known, but we have the inventory of his estate, which amounted to a little over $800.[17]

The door Levi designed for the Burling House has been preserved in Natchez as the main entrance to Texada Tavern. Written on the reverse side of a section of paneling is an eerie inscription by Ann Weeks. Her name, the date (March 23, 1823) and the names of their children are included with the following: "Look at this when I am dead and gone and remember you must all die."[18] Ann married a man named Dan Harris some time after 1823.[19]

NOTES ON THE AFTERWORD

[1]Mildred Blewett McGehee, "Levi Weeks, Early Nineteenth-Century Architect" (Master's thesis, University of Delaware, Winterthur Program, 1976), 1.

[2]McGehee, "Levi Weeks," 2.

[3]McGehee, "Levi Weeks," 1.

[4]McGehee, "Levi Weeks," 2.

[5]McGehee, "Levi Weeks," 4.

[6]McGehee, "Levi Weeks," 5.

[7]Thomas Weeks to Levi Weeks, 11 January 1808, Levi Weeks and Family Letters Collection, Mississippi Department of Archives and History.

[8]McGehee, "Levi Weeks," 5.

[9]Ezra Weeks to Levi Weeks, 17 July 1812, Levi Weeks and Family Letters Collection, Mississippi Department of Archives and History.

[10]McGehee, "Levi Weeks," 7.

[11]Mildred Blewett McGehee, "Auburn in Natchez" in *Antiques* (March 1977): 551.

[12]Levi Weeks to Epaphras Hoyt, 27 September 1812, Levi Weeks and Family Letters Collection.

[13]McGehee, "Levi Weeks," 42.

[14]Katie D. McClutchie, "Information on Levi Weeks," Levi Weeks and Family Letters Collection, 4.
[15]McGehee, "Levi Weeks," 14.
[16]McClutchie, 5-6.
[17]McClutchie, 9.
[18]McGehee, "Levi Weeks," 64.
[19]McClutchie, 9.

BIBLIOGRAPHY FOR THE AFTERWORD

Chisolm, J. Julian. *History of the First Presbyterian Church of Natchez, Mississippi.* Natchez: McDonald's Printers & Pub., 1972.

James, D. Clayton. *Antebellum Natchez.* Baton Rouge: Louisiana State University Press, 1968.

Kane, Harnett T. *Natchez.* New York: William Morrow & Co., 1947.

Levi Weeks and Family Letters Collection. Mississippi Department of Archives and History, Jackson, Miss.

Mary Ann Irvine Papers. Mississippi Department of Archives and History, Jackson, Miss.

McGehee, Mildred Blewett. "Levi Weeks, Early Nineteenth-Century Architect." Master's thesis, University of Delaware, Winterthur Program, 1976.

________."Auburn in Natchez" in *Antiques* (March 1977): 546-553.

Miller, Mary Warren and Ronald W. Miller. *The Great Houses of Natchez.* Jackson, Miss. and London: University Press of Mississippi, 1968.

Pishel, Robert Gordon. *Natchez, Museum City of the Old South.* Tulsa: Magnolia Publishing Co., 1959.

APPENDIX

This letter, written on September 27, 1812, from Levi to Epaphras Hoyt (an historian who held many civil and military offices in Deerfield) provides some insight into Levi's character, social position and education, and contains interesting details about the history, population and agriculture of Natchez in the early part of the nineteenth century. Original spelling has been retained.

Natchez, 27th Sept. 1812

Ep. Hoyt, Esq.
Deerfield, Mass.

Dear Sir

Your favor of the 22d ultimo was duly received by the last mail. It is with regret I am compeld. to apologize for not having answered your queries of Jany. last. My means of collecting materials have been but small as you shall hear by and by, and a train of circumstances I can hardly tell why, has prevented me from sooner complying but on opening your last I imagined that a part of those circumstances might be attributed to neglect (which God knows I never intended) I immediately determined to set about it.

Should I find materials in my head and time to disembark them you shall have a copy as fast as I can write,—but first it may not be amiss to inform you of the sphere in which I walk and the necessity of employing the most of my time in my vocations. As to society it is but a few families that I visit, those are of the first standing—My employment is the superintendance of a large brick house and a brick Presbyterian Church as architect. Those buildings together with a cabinet and chair shop that I carry on solely without even a foreman that can be depended on you will readily believe must occupy the most of my time, especially when I have to board my shop men as is the custom of the country—from 10 to 18 in family and nobody to attend to that part but a negro cook. I have also been employed the season past to give plans for an Hospital and Banking house which with the stupidity I had to contend with took much time—do not however expect system from me in communications—I shall relate facts as they exist generally leaving them for you to make your own deductions—and If I should sometimes contradict Doct. Morso you will please not expose me, as I might be thought an Heretic but I assure you he is frequently incorrect—and sometimes altogether false. I do not blame the Doct. for this, because he gave such as he received and this country has been so many times shifted from one government to another, it is no wonder that false facts should have been related, were it for no other purpose than to prejudice the mind for political motives. For instances such as that the cypress tree is poison! It is well known all the swamps of this country abound with this valuable timber and to tell strangers that it is poison, would have a fine effect in keeping back or retarding population. The cypress is no more poison than is the hemlock or spruce of your contry [*sic*]. Those swamps and their immediate vicinity are esteemed unhealthy in the hot season—The reason is evident. They are more or less overflowed by the waters of the Miss. until July when the hot season commences. Then takes place the putrefaction of thousands of vegetables of the growth of the preceding season, and the air is uncommonly humid together with the millions of huge mosquetoes [*sic*] who attack cattle with such ferocity that they will run lowing out of the wood. These are sufficient reasons I think why the swamps are unhealthy or poison, if you please—but when they are levied up so that the water cannot go on them and put under cultivation they are as healthy as the meadows of Deerfield, and any part of them as productive and if possible more fertile than Poges Hole. You speak of Mr. Shults or Schultz. I have not seen any of his writings. I expect they have not found their way here, indeed should doubt whether they would be well received, if he has given such a description as you mention of the ladies and still more doubt whether it is advisable to bring the book himself. Believe me, such scribblers are not the proper characters to describe the better part of society. A traveller who is ever so capable of writing and has not had a considerable residence in the place could not possibly be correctly informed—for who would be his acquaintances? Most likely an ignorant tavern keeper or the more worthless gamester. How should they or any acquaintance a man could immediately make give the true character of the people? It is certain that Mr. Schultz could not have proCured [*sic*] such information from any man of standing in the country, and if he wrote from experience his company must have been the common prostitutes—for such are the habits and customs and such is the care and education or call it what you please that I have never known or heard of an instance of bastardy in a respectable family since I came to the country nor have I ever noticed that married ladies behaved with more levity than the unmarried.

Geography gives you the outlines of this territory—

The city of Natchez is situated on a bluff of about 200 feet perpendicular height from high water mark of the Miss. River, about 300 miles by the course of the river from New Orleans, 150 in a direct line—100 miles from Lake Ponchartrain, 50 miles from the line of demarkation of Florida. The bluff is very irregular sometimes approaching the river itself, then receding leaves a plane which sometimes overflowed in May and June and the river banks constantly liable to fall. More than ten acres have sunk and altogether disappeared in four years, so that in a short time the river will probably sweep along the whole bluff in which there is now large excavations of more than 100 feet in depth a little below the town.

The Act of Incorporation makes the city one mile each way from a center point, but it is not regularly laid off, only 30 squares of about 300 feet each, each square containing 4 lots. Some of those lots are again subdivided to suit convenience. There is a lawn left in front of these squares facing the river, from the edge of the bluff perhaps the space is 350 yards, which is set out with trees of locust and Pride of China. This land was given to the city by Congress upon the express condition that it should remain a common and ornamented with trees.

The face of the land on which the town is built and its vicinity is very uneven. You are constantly ascending and descending as you pass through in any direction. The streets running northeast and southwest and at right angles. There is but one road by which a team can pass down the bluff to the river, this winds down in a serpentine direction but is still of quick descent. The houses are extremely irregular and for the most part temporary things. But of late a number of good houses have been built. I last year built an excellent two story brick house 2d rate fireproof—in the vicinity of town there is a number of Gentlemen's Seats who have plantations more distant in bottoms, etc. The brick house I am now building is just without the city line, and is designed for the most magnificent building in the territory.* The body of this house is 60 by 45 feet with a portico of 31 feet projecting 12 feet supported by 4 Ionic collumns [*sic*] with the Corinthian entabliture—the ceiling vaulted, the house two stories, with a geometrical staircase to ascend to the second story. This is the first house in the territory on which was ever attempted any of the orders of architecture. The site is one of those peculiar situations which combines all of the delight of romance—the pleasures of rurality and the approach of sublimity. I am the more particular in describing this seat not only to give you an idea of the progress of improvement but to inform you what you will hear with pleasure—that the owner of it is a Yankey [*sic*]—a native of our own state Mass. and is now in Boston on a visit. His name—Lyman Harding—received his education at Cambridge, came to this country more pennyless than myself—his celebrity as an attorney and counsellor at law has no competition in the Territory—he has a little son (his only child) now in Boston. He has amassed a large fortune, owns an extensive sugar plantation in the Attakapas on the Bayou Texche [sic]. You will excuse this digression for I love to think and speak of my own countrymen who will not let the saucy Virginian and supercilious Carolinian ride them down.

On the plane below the bluff there is a great number of small houses which accommodate boatmen and the like, and where the filth of creation reside. This place is called *Under the Hill* and in further speaking of Natchez I shall distinguish this place in that way. I give the following from recollections which therefore can not be exaggerated but expect will be found to be pretty correct—

*In the lines that follow, Levi Weeks is describing Auburn.

Mechanics, Manufacturers, Men of Profession and Public Establishments in Natchez

4 Taylor Shops
6 Blacksmiths do.
4 Sadlers do.
6 Carpenters do.
5 Cabinet Makers do.
1 Coach and Sign Painter
3 House Painters
4 Hatter Shops
2 Tinner do.
5 Boot and Shoe do.
1 Trunk Maker
1 Book Binder
1 Wagon Maker
1 Coach Maker
1 Nail Factory
3 Barbers
5 Brick Yards
2 Butchers
5 Bakers
5 Gold and Silver Smiths
1 Confectioner and distiller
4 Master Brick Layers
2 Plasterers
1 Horse Mill for grinding corn
12 Water Carts
8 Practicing Physicians
7 Lawyers

On the road up the hill

2 Catalene shops in one of which is a shoe maker

6 Public Inns
5 Warehouses
1 Reading room and coffee house
20 Mercantile houses or dry goods stores
4 grocery stores
2 wholesale common stores
17 Catalene Shops or small stores where a little of everything is sold.
2 Vendue and common stores
1 Bank called the Bank of the Miss., capital $500,000
2 Windsor Chair Makers

Under the Hill

1 Tavern, the "Kentucky"
2 Blacksmith shops
18 Catalene Shops, porter houses, etc.
1 Incorporated Mechanical Society

3 Printing offices issuing weekly papers	1 Free Mason Lodge
	6 Magistrates
2 Porter Houses	4 English Schools

The town has been supplied altogether by the waters from the Miss. until of late there is 3 wells and a great number of cisterns introduced by your humble servant, which is found to almost supercede the necessity for water carts.

The Public Buildings are a City Hall and Market House, a Catholic Church, a small Methodist meeting house, and engine house and a new church I am now erecting, the cornerstone of which was laid about the first inst. with the following inscription etched by myself on steel—

"This church designed for the Presbyterian worship of God, founded by donations of individuals of Natchez and its vicinity A.D. 1812 Samuel Brooks, John Henderson, John Steele, Joseph Forman, Lewis Evans, Lyman Harding, James McIntosh and Thos. L. Scroop, commissioners; Lewis Evans, contractor, Levi Weeks, architect; Swan and Williams, masons."

The place was lade in the stone and covered with cement that will keep it from corroding, and with a well conducted ceremony—assisted by the parson, was laid down.

There is the remains of several old fortifications—all now wholly neglected—The people are of all kinds and of almost all nations, from every state in the Union as well as French, Spanish, Creoles, English, Irish, Dutch, Swedes and Danes and above all—Ethiopians! Although this place was settled very early by the French, it has experienced such a rapid change of masters alternately from and to the French, Spanish and English that when the U. S. got possession it had to undergo all the vicissitudes of a new settled country—for villains from all parts will seek refuge on the frontier and as the country becomes peopled in process of time they give place to better inhabitants. A variety of causes, however, renders this process rather slow in this place, although it is perceptibly progressing. One of those causes are that a great many who visit the country come as mere speculators to seek fortune and take it away, imagining they can find a more salubrious climate!

Another cause is as evident as the one last mentioned that the Government is at present but a mob, a few intriguing individuals will caress the vulgar and it is the vulgar alone that now governs. Thank God for one good thing the war will do, that is, take away and perhaps destroy a horde of as great vagabonds as ever existed and we may probably get better men in place by those miscreants not being able to come and vote. The city was formerly governed by a Mayor, Recorder, and Council who also held a monthly court to try petty causes and appeals from magistrates, but since the mob government commenced those officers were put down and the place is now governed by a president and six selectmen—the president is the chief magistrate—all this to make the ignorant believe their situation is bettered, when in truth it is ten times worse. Those intriguers are eternally Virginians for leaders and Irishmen for actors with some French cut-throat for an interpreter, and astonishing to relate, some scoundrel Yankeys [*sic*] have caught the Sulivanian fire and like N. Hampton Shepherds are driving their flocks along the road to anarchy—such a man—I expect was Schultz who perhaps visited the men at present in power in this city and though I blush to relate one of them is a Yankey [*sic*] by the name of Burt—a sadler from N. Hampton, not one of them a single instance excepted that has ever had an opportunity of being acquainted with the respectable part of Society, and the

President himself lives publicly with a common prostitute. Burt's wife has been publicly known as the same character, as well as the wives of three others of the selectmen. Heavens! What are we to come to, if governed by such people! Let me ask if our Nation is not governed much in the same way?

The war I think will put out of the way the very characters that it ought and they will be no loss to society, although a great portion of the people here as well as in your country equally disapprove the measures taken by the general government—of this I may speak more fully in a future No. Do not think, however, that because such men are in power we have no good society. There are numerous families which they never did, nor ever will they approach. After filling this sheet with some further observations, I will take up your queries more circumstancially.

There is perhaps no soil or climate better adapted for the production of esculents for the table than that of the state of La. and Miss. Territory, with a very little care and attention from a small piece of ground a family may be supplied with some one or other of various garden vegetables, all the year round. It would be fruitless for me to say I could enumerate the half of those plants that succeed in this country. Should Providence ever place me in situation to have a little leisure I intend keeping a diary, but as yet I have done it except when I was traveling and even that is now lost in the Homochitto River, where I was also very near remaining in an attempt to swim it with an ungovernable Spanish horse.

A few of the numerous kinds of esculents follow: Peas and Beans a great variety—Parsley and put herbs of all kinds—Lettuce—Endive—Fennel, sorrel—salsafy, spinach, asparagus, artichokes are cultivated with great success, cucumbers, musk, cantaloupe and water melons [*sic*] a great variety, pumpkins, squash, and gourds, cabbages of all kinds, savoys (It is presumable that the cauliflower and broccoli have not had a fair trial) Radishes, horse radish, turnips, carrots parsnips, white and red beets, the latter of which grows with remarkable luxuriance. Celery, ocra [*sic*], the eggplant, Jerusalem artichoke, capsicums or red pepper from 8 to 12 different kinds and of different flavors from the sweet to the pungency of kian-garlic, leeks, salad, onions do not succeed very well—sweet potatoes in great perfection, good irish potatoes if the seed is annually renewed from the north. It may not be amiss to notice here that all top and bulbous-rooted plants are better if the seed be annually renewed which is easily done from Penn. and Ohio. The fruits are chiefly figs, nectarines, almonds, peaches, quinces, pomgranates, plums and strawberries. The pear and apricot have been tried. Vines are not generally cultivated, but if they were wanted, be found to succeed admirably. The currant and raspberry do not succeed well. The blackberry and dewberry are indigenous and found in their greatest perfection. The orange does not come to perfection much above New Orleans. It is said the olive may be cultivated to advantage in the Attakapas district. The apple tree bears tolerably well, but the tree is not lasting, nor will the fruit keep any length of time. Many and great improvements might be made in the arts of culinary gardening and the cultivation of fruit trees. They are yet in their infancy, but bid fair at no distant period to exhibit an exuberant maturity. The wild fruits are very numerous; then there are of the nut kind the pecan, walnuts of various kinds, hickory and chinquepin. Beside these are mulberries, cherries, papaws, crabapples, grapes in great abundance, plums (a species of which called the Chickesaw [*sic*] plum is of a superior quality), persimmons which become delicious without frost, and a variety of wild berries.

Now for I thought to have commenced the answer of your enquiries with all the conscious dignity of a man [in] possession [of] a fund of wealth commensurate with his highest ambition, but I find myself so "unequal to the task" that I shrink into littleness at the thought, and number of questions are involuntarily put to me by my secret monitor—How have I spent my time? Why have I not kept a diary and notes which would not have taken more than 5 or 10 minutes in a day? Are you at this advanced period to answer simple questions, I don't know? and the like—to all which some answer might be given but would be wholly uninteresting to you. I shall therefore proceed by a short cut road to a conclusion.

The breadth of the Miss. at Natchez is about ¾ of a mile, its depth from 20 to 30 fathoms. The velocity of its current is 4 miles an hour on an average. The Miss. is very uniform in breadth and strength of current, but there is many exceptions of little moment while it is within its banks, but when it is high its breadth is hardly known.

You may travel 50 miles westwardly in small batteau and its banks are almost everywhere overflowing. Some of the waters that run out of it return again and some pursue another course and roll through vast tracts of country to the gulf. The country opposite Natchez—for considerable distance above as well as all the way to the ocean is checkered with numerous streams some of which receive their supply from the Miss. and other from the regions of the west and north. This country can not be surpassed for fertility. Some of it requires leveeing to keep out the back waters, but Nature has formed so many canals called here Bayou's that almost every plantation has or may have the benefit of them, and where any deficiency may happen might easily be supplied by Art at a small expense. It appears to me that Egypt itself can have no pretentions to equal this country. On this side of the river the high land commences sooner. The face of it is rolling with rather a thin soil, but some excellent land not with standing.

A Kentucky Boat which carries 60 thousand or 30 tons. . .[Diagram of boat here]. . .These are called a "Kentucky Boat" but they are no means confined to that state. They are made in the states of N. Y., Pa. and all the other states and territories on the western waters—They are, however, distinguishable by us from their timber or some little difference in their formation which is by no means essential, their structure is so coarse that they cost only from 60 to 70 dollars when they are made, and are made use of as firewood when they get to their place of destination.

In these boats are brought all the surplus produce of the western country to a market either here or New Orleans or to some other place on the lower Miss. I can not tell the number that descends annually—it is, however, from 4 to 6000.

Their produce is corn, bacon, pork, lard, beef, hogs, cattle, horses, sheep, venison, cordage, hemp, bagging, cloth of flax and tow, beeswax, tallow—in fine, every necessary of life—but since the price of our staple has been so much reduced they have found but ordinary markets.

The wild animals are much the same here as in the state of Ohio except some few of the Tyger or Leopard and the wild cat more numerous—the furs are good for nothing. Deer is the principle game which is very plenty. The country east of the Miss. after passing from 12 to 30 miles from the river is fine land nearly all the way to the Tombigbee with here and there a fertile spot—of course the population is very thin, but from the river to the pines there is a good portion of land under cultivation. There is, however, more or less settlements all the way to that place.

With respect to meteorological observations I am not able to give you any satisfactory account. Governor Sargeant who has the best aparatus [*sic*] of this kind keeps his observations in a family diary—he has long promised to give me a transcript of such as I enquired for, but he is so afflicted with the gout that I doubt much of ever getting it. The mercury is never over 98 and very seldom so low as the freezing point. In the month of June last the highest was 92 and lowest 55; in July the highest 86 and the lowest 62 so you will see that it is not in extremes of heat and cold we live in, but the average warmth is much greater than your country.

You ask me about the late William Dunbar, Esqr. This was a truly respectable man, a Scotsman by birth, came here in early time and acumulated [*sic*] a large property—his philosophical, astronomical and chemical aparatus was superior to any that has ever been brought to the country. I can not describe them—I was introduced to this gentleman soon after my arrival but he was then laboring under the painful disease (the stone) which has since put an end to a long and useful life—I am intimate with two of the gentlemen that married daughters of his and have frequent invitations to visit them but they live 12 miles from town and the seat of the late William Dunbar about the same distance and not very near the other gentlemen. I have never taken the time to make my intended visit. The whole aparatus is easy of access. There is one son who tho young it is said has a natural turn for the pursuits of his father—Mr. Dunbar certainly deserved great credit for traveling so far as he did in the field of science in a country where he could not possibly have a companion—

Well, I have, contrary to my intention when I sat down, began on the fifth sheet. I begin to suspect you are wearied with my dulness and proliscity but since I have got to the work I could continue for five times five sheets and then appear more like beginning than when the first sheet was written. This however, will be the last I shall trouble you with this mail. Business will sometime pop into my head and cause blunders in spite of me. Those you will please overlook. Among all this work I have not been polite enough to thank you for the interesting information you gave me. Be assured, Sir, I will ever be grateful to you for information on any subject that interests my Friends or my Country.

So Detroit has fallen. Great God. Is it possible that we have been so weak after all this blustering as to let the first army in so short a time fall into the hands of an unprepared enemy! People here are very clamorous against Genl. Hale and declare him a traitor and is it possible?—I am not prepared to determine—be it as it may, it is a dreadful stroke. The whole western savages are let loose on our frontiers and God only knows where they will stop.

Now for the last and most important query—"Where can a man live the most happy?" This subject combines so many other important questions that I hardly know how to commence answering of it, but presuming that you only meant to enquire of me the different ways to make money in the different places I have visited—I shall only relate some facts and draw such positive deductions as necessarily attend those that I shall relate, combined with others that is only acquired by habit and cannot be expressed with drawing the subject too lengthy for my sheet—The state of Ohio is without exception the best poor man's country in the world because they have no slaves and of course more quality. There can be no soil under Heaven more luxuriant for the earth produces the most suckulent plants year after year as thick as they can stand without any seeming diminution from want of strength of soil. Therefore a man who will work a little can live well. The climate is mild and well adapted to the growth of all the necessaries of life. Therefore they need but little money. Manufactories are there improving; they will therefore be nearly independent in a short time.

Kentucky enjoys nearly the same advantages but I do not like the people as well, for the most part they are from S. Carolina and Va. They were brought up among slaves, and their manners especially of the lower class is very disgusting. There is a tolerable good society in Lexington but not equal to that of Cincinnati, nor is the society in the latter place so good as Marietta, but the country parts of both (Ohio and Kentucky) is undesirable for a man of breeding to live in. It would be a life of penance.

So much for that country. But I confess a more Southern climate suits my ideas better, because nearly all that do hold lands or where there is a plantation opened, there will generally be found some decently educated people who are hospitable as well as polite and agreeable, and a man without a family can do very well for a while if he has no money until he can get some respectable employment. I requires [*sic*] the forst [*sic*] of some [? illegible] for a person without money to get a respectable place for making money, especially if he has a family, but when that situation is once obtained by a persevering hand it never fails of success.

There is some little prejudices of the Yankeys [*sic*] that must be overcome, such as aversion to slavery and the like. Another pretty serious consideration is that all who migrate from a cold to a hot climate must expect to undergo what is called seasoning—that is—have a feveer [*sic*] perhaps the ague with it, afterward the Miss. itch which is an eruption of the skin over the whole body, but this itch is more universal with children than with adults. I do not think any danger in this seasoning for I am so well used to it in my family that I cure them without any medical aid. There is in this country all the advantages [? illegible] Ohio and a greater variety of luxuries.

A man may commence business with less money in Ohio than here—in the same circle of society but he would not have the opportunity perhaps of accumulating so fast. I speak of a man of family, for as to a young man if his appearance and behavior comport with a gentleman—it is not enquired if he has money. You see, I have nearly gone through my paper and said but little for so interesting a subject. I will endeavor to give you some further hints in my next, which perhaps you may find on opening the next mail. Meanwhile permit me to subscribe myself your friend and obedt. servant.

L. Weeks

Letter reprinted courtesy of the Levi Weeks and Family Letters Collection, Mississippi Department of Archives and History, Jackson, Mississippi.

NOTES

[1]John Allen Krout and Dixon Ryan Fox, *The Completion of Independence* (New York: Macmillan Co., 1944), 46.

[2]Edward S. Gould, "The Manhattan Well Murder," *Harper's New Monthly Magazine* 44, (December 1871 to May 1872): 924.

[3]*Moreau de St Mery's American Journey: 1793-1798,* ed. and trans. Kenneth and Anna M. Roberts (New York: Doubleday & Co., Inc., 1947), 166.

[4]I.N. Phelps Stokes, *Iconography of Manhattan Island* (1926; reprint, New York: Arno Press, 1967), 5:1204.

[5]Frank Monaghan and Marvin Lowenthal, *This Was New York* (New York: Doubleday, Doran & Co., Inc., 1943), 204.

[6]Allan McLane Hamilton, *The Intimate Life of Alexander Hamilton* (London: Duckworth & Co., 1910), 363.

[7]Richard B. Morris, *Alexander Hamilton and the Founding of the Nation* (New York: Dial Press, 1957), 538.

[8]Milton Lomask, *Aaron Burr: The Years from Princeton to Vice President, 1756-1805* (New York: Farrar, Straus & Giroux, 1979), 347.

[9]*New York Gazette and General Advertiser,* 6 January 1800.

[10]*Commercial Advertiser,* 6 January 1800.

[11]Julius Goebel, Jr., ed., *The Law Practice of Alexander Hamilton* (New York: Columbia University Press, 1964), 1:697.

[12]*New York Gazette and General Advertiser,* 10 January 1800.

[13]Goebel, 687.

[14]Lomask, 129-130.

[15]Lomask, 239-240.

[16]Sidney I. Pomerantz, *New York, An American City: 1783-1803* (New York: Columbia University Press, 1938), 462.

[17]Mrs Martha Lamb and Mrs Burton Harrison, *History of the City of New York* (New York: A.S. Barnes Co., 1877), 3:440.
[18]Lamb and Harrison, 3:455.
[19]Lomask, 116.
[20]Goebel, 698.
[21]Pomerantz, 281.
[22]Stokes, 1357.
[23]Lomask, 227.
[24]Lomask, 228.
[25]Stokes, 1361.
[26]*Report of the Manhattan Company* (New York: John Furman, 1799), 29-30.
[27]John W. Degraw, "Recollections of Early New York," in *The Evening Post,* 7 October 1882.
[28]Lomask, 229.
[29]Thomas E.V. Smith, *The City of New York in the Year of Washington's Inauguration* (1889; reprint, Riverside, Connecticut: Chatham Press, 1972), 232.
[30]*Commercial Advertiser,* 2 April 1800.
[31]James Hardie, *An Impartial Account of the Trial of Mr Levi Weeks, for the Supposed Murder of Miss Julianna Elmore Sands, at a Court Held in the City of New York,* (New York: N. McFarlane, 31 March 1800).
[32]Lamb and Harrison, 2:279.
[33]Lamb and Harrison, 2:299.
[34]Lomask, 85.
[35]James Parton, *The Life and Times of Aaron Burr* (1858; reprint, New York: Johnson Reprint Corp., 1967), 149.
[36]This account of the trial (and all of the testimony in the chapters that follow) is taken from William Coleman, *Report of the Trial of Levi Weeks, On an Indictment for the Murder of Gulielma Sands, on Monday the thirty-first day of March, and Tuesday the first day of April, 1800. Taken in short hand by the clerk of the court* (New York: John Furman, 1800). All irregularities in grammar, spelling and punctuation have been preserved. "Elma," for example, is often called "Elmore," Lorena Forrest, a witness, also appears as Lorena Forest, "show" is spelled "shew," and the family homestead is called Cornwall and New-Cornwall. The British spelling has also been preserved. Variations of fact appear in Coleman's transcript as well. The location of Elma's bedroom,

for instance, differs according to which witness is testifying (compare the testimonies of Catherine Ring, Isaac Hatfield, Elias Ring and Betsy Watkins).

[37]*Discipline of the Yearly Meeting of Friends, held in New-York for the State of New-York and Parts Adjacent* (New York: Collins & Perkins, 1810).

[38]Jean Pierre Brissot de Warville, "Comfortable Philadelphia," (1788), in *American History told by Contemporaries,* Albert Bushnell Hart ed., (New York: Macmillan Co., 1910), 3:37.

[39]Tea was the third meal of the day, customarily taken between seven and eight in the evening.

[40]It was important for the prosecuting attorney to establish this point: a modest woman was entitled to society's protection; not so, the other kind. Colden's grandfather, the first Cadwallader Colden, once wrote to his granddaughters devoting the entire letter to the subject of modesty. Of all the qualities which would gain for them society's esteem, modesty, he wrote, was foremost.

Elma's behavior was modest, according to a neighbor whose letter was published in the newspaper at the time Elma's body was found: "Her temper was mild and tranquil, her manners artless and tender; her conversation ever chaste and innocent. She was one of those virtuous characters against whom the tongue of slander never moves." From David T. Valentine, *Manuals of the Corporation of the City of New York* (New York: Common Council of the City of New York, 1861), 631.

[41]According to the *New York Gazette and General Advertiser* of 6 January 1800: "The father of the young lady, Mr —— Sands was an eminent preacher of the Society of Friends, and died some time ago in England. Her mother, an aged and venerable matron, at present resides in the vicinity of New Windsor in this State, and is so infirm that, though notice has been sent to her with respect to her daughter's fate, it was not expected that she could be able to attend the funeral."

[42]*Dictionary of American Biography,* ed. Dumas Malone (New York: Charles Scribner's Sons, 1933), 6:314.

[43]Parton, 148.

[44]Benjamin Franklin, "Characteristics of America," (1784), in Hart, *American History told by Contemporaries,* 3:26.

[45]Pomerantz, 305-307. A letter to the *Daily Advertiser* in 1800 questioned whether "this absurd custom" of not lighting the lamps when there was a moon should be followed on those nights when the "moon rises, tho' it be ever so late;" and suggested that the lamps be lit on all nights. But this idea was too radical for the times, and nothing was done about it.

[46]Goebel, 703.

[47]*Commercial Advertiser,* 6 January 1800.

[48]Milton Helpern, M.D., and Bernard Knight, M.D., *Autopsy* (New York: St. Martin's Press, 1977), 7-10.

[49]Parton, 148. According to Parton, in Burr's later years he was said to have boasted of saving a man from the gallows by a clever arrangement of candles.

[50]John Church Hamilton, *History of the Republic of the United States of America as Traced in the Writings of Alexander Hamilton and his Contemporaries* (Philadelphia: Appleton, 1864), 7:745-747.

[51]Allan McLane Hamilton, 186-187.

[52]Goebel, 704.

[53]David T. Valentine, *Manuals of the Corporation of the City of New York* (New York: Common Council of the City of New York, 1861), 631.

[54]David Longworth, *A Brief Narrative of the Trial for the Bloody and Mysterious Murder of the Unfortunate Young Woman in the Famous Manhattan Well.* Taken in Short Hand by a Gentleman of the Bar. (New York, 1800).

[55]Hardie, vi.

[56]David Willard, *History of Greenfield* (Greenfield, Massachusetts: Kneeland & Eastman, 1838), 164.

[57]*Commercial Advertiser,* 2 April 1800.

[58]Willard, 163.

[59]Valentine, 629.

[60][Keturah Connah], *Guilty or not Guilty, The True Story of the Manhattan Well* (New York: Carleton Publishers, 1870).

[61]Gould, 924-928. Edward S. Gould's own death was the subject of a lawsuit in which a jury failed to follow a judge's directive. Gould, by then a man of eighty, was killed when he tried to cross the street at Broadway and Park Place. He stood in the street with his hand raised to the traffic, and witnesses testified that the driver of a truck ignored Gould's signal, drove over him, and continued at the same rate of

speed until he was stopped by a policeman. The charge against the truckman was manslaughter, and the story was carried on March 19, 1885, in *The New York Times,* under the caption "A Miscarriage of Justice":

. . . The defense was that the horse was hard of mouth, the day very cold, and as the driver had left his gloves at home he was unable to stop the animal. Assistant District Attorney Bedford urged that, as the driver knew the horse perfectly well before he started out, it was evidence of criminal negligence that he left his gloves at home. Much to the surprise of the court and almost everybody else the jury acquitted Troeger [the truckman].

Judge Cowling said to Troeger: 'I don't know what to say in this case. If anyone ever deserved punishment you did, and I hope that in future when an old gentleman raises his hand as you are driving down on him, you will come to a standstill instead of driving on, and after knocking him down continuing to drive on until you are brought to a standstill.'

At this point in the Judge's remarks the sixth juror, John A. Ebnendorf, stood up and said: 'Why, your Honor, I once did the same thing as this man under similar circumstances.' 'Well!' returned Judge Cowling, severely, 'I am very sorry to hear you make such an acknowledgment in court. I think you ought to be ashamed of it.' Then, continuing his remarks to Troeger, he said: '. . . I never like to take exception to the verdict of a jury, but it seems to me that in this case there was certainly a grave miscarriage of justice.'

[62]Lomask, 91.

[63]Broadus Mitchell, *Alexander Hamilton: A Concise Biography* (New York: Oxford University Press, 1976), 310.

[64]Robert Hendrickson, *Hamilton: 1789-1804* (New York: Mason/Charter, 1976), 2:583.

[65]Samuel H. Wandell and Meade Minnigerode, *Aaron Burr* (New York: G.P. Putnam's Sons, 1927), 134.

[66]Broadus Mitchell, *Alexander Hamilton, The National Adventure: 1788-1804* (New York: Macmillan Co., 1962), 2:378.

[67]Herbert S. Parmet and Marie B. Hecht, *Aaron Burr, Portrait of an Ambitious Man* (New York: Macmillan Co., 1967), 147.

[68]Goebel, 701.

[69]Goebel, 702.

[70]Goebel, 703.

[71]Goebel, 702.

[72]Dr George D. Lundberg, letter to editor, 8 August 1988.

[73]Robert Bard, letter to author, 15 August 1988.

[74]Meyer Berger, "About New York," *The New York Times,* 10 October 1957.

[75]Wandell and Minnigerode, 135.

[76]Lamb and Harrison, 3:453.

[77]*Dictionary of American Biography,* 6:313.

[78]Allan Nevins, *The Evening Post* (New York: Boni and Liveright, 1922), 163.

[79]*Dictionary of American Biography,* 5:609.

[80]*Report of the Trial of Richard D. Croucher on an Indictment for a Rape on Margaret Miller, People v. R.D. Croucher, 8 July 1800,* from Minutes of the Court of Oyer and Terminer and General Gaol Delivery, 1796-1801 (Readex Microfilm Evans 38373).

[81]John Church Hamilton, 747.

[82]*Story of the Old Homestead: 1732-1932* (Cornwall, New York: The Two Hundredth Anniversary Committee, 1932).

[83]*Records of the Monthly Meeting of the Society of Friends* (Havilland Records Room, New York City).

[84]William Wade Hinshaw, *Encyclopedia of Quaker Genealogy* (Ann Arbor, Michigan: Edwards Brothers, Inc., 1940), 3:278.

BIBLIOGRAPHY

Baker, Liva. "The Defense of Levi Weeks" in *American Bar Association Journal* 63 (June, 1977): 818-823.

Baldick, Robert. *The Duel.* New York: Clarkson N. Potter, Inc., 1965.

Berber, John. *Historical Collections of the State of New York.* New York: Austin & Co., 1851.

Berridge, Virginia and Griffin Edwards. *Opium and the People.* New York: St. Martin's Press, 1961.

Booth, Mary Louise. *History of the City of New York.* 3 vols. New York: Clark & Meeker, 1856.

Bowne, Eliza Southgate. *A Girl's Life Eighty Years Ago.* 1887. Reprint. Williamstown, Mass.: Corner House Publishers, 1980.

Coleman, William. *Report of the Trial of Levi Weeks, On an Indictment for the Murder of Gulielma Sands, on Monday the thirty-first day of March, and Tuesday the first day of April, 1800. Taken in short hand by the clerk of the court.* New York: John Furman, 1800.

Degraw, John W. "Recollections of Early New York" in *The Evening Post* (7 October 1882).

Delaney, Edmund T. *New York's Greenwich Village.* Barre, Mass.: Barre Publishers, 1967.

Discipline of the Yearly Meeting of Friends, held in New-York For the State of New-York and Parts Adjacent. New York: Collins & Perkins, 1810.

Dunshee, Kenneth Holcomb. *As You Pass By.* New York: Hastings House, 1952.

Earle, Alice Moore. *Two Centuries of Costume.* New York: Macmillan Co., 1903.

Ellis, Edward Robb. *The Epic of New York City.* New York: Coward-McCann, Inc., 1966.

Fay, Theodore S. *Norman Leslie.* 2 vols. New York: Harper & Bros., 1835. [First edition published anonymously.]

Friedman, Lawrence M. *A History of American Law.* New York: Simon & Schuster, 1973.

Gilder, Rodman. *The Battery.* Boston: Houghton Mifflin Co., 1956.

Goebel, Julius, Jr., ed. *The Law Practice of Alexander Hamilton.* 2 vols. New York: Columbia University Press, 1964.

Gould, Edward S. "The Manhattan Well Murder, December 22, 1799" in *Harper's New Monthly Magazine* 44 (December 1871 to May 1872): 924-928.

[Connah, Keturah]. *Guilty or Not Guilty, The True Story of the Manhattan Well.* New York: Carleton Publishers, 1870.

Hamilton, Allan McLane. *The Intimate Life of Alexander Hamilton.* London: Duckworth & Co., 1910.

Hamilton, John Church. *History of the Republic of the United States of America as Traced in the Writings of Alexander Hamilton and his Contemporaries.* Vol. 7. Philadelphia: Appleton, 1864.

Handlin, Oscar, ed. *This Was America.* New York: Harper & Row, 1949.

Hardie, James. *An Impartial Account of the Trial of Mr Levi Weeks, for the Supposed Murder of Miss Julianna Elmore Sands, at a Court Held in the City of New York.* New York: N. McFarlane, 31 March 1800.

Harlow, Alvin F. *Old Bowery Days.* New York: D. Appleton & Co., 1931.

Hart, Albert Bushnell, ed. *American History told by Contemporaries.* Vol. 3. New York: Macmillan Co., 1910.

Hayter, Alethea. *Opium and the Romantic Imagination.* Berkley and Los Angeles: University of California Press, 1968.

Helpern, Milton, M.D. and Bernard Knight, M.D. *Autopsy.* New York: St. Martin's Press, 1977.

Hendrickson, Robert. *Hamilton: 1789-1804.* 2 vols. New York: Mason/Charter, 1976.

Hinshaw, William Wade. *Encyclopedia of Quaker Genealogy.* Vol. 3. Ann Arbor, Mich.: Edwards Bros., Inc., 1940.

Jones, Pamela. *Under the City Streets.* New York: Holt, Rinehart & Winston, 1978.

Katz, Herbert and Marjorie Katz. *Museums, U.S.A.* New York: Doubleday & Co., Inc., 1965.

Kouwenhoven, John A. *The Columbia Historical Portrait of New York.* New York: Harper & Row, 1953.

Krout, John Allen and Dixon Ryan Fox. *The Completion of Independence.* New York: Macmillan Co., 1944.

Lamb, Mrs. Martha and Mrs. Burton Harrison. *History of the City of New York.* 3 vols. New York: A.S. Barnes Co., 1877.

Lomask, Milton. *Aaron Burr: The Years from Princeton to Vice President, 1756-1805.* New York: Farrar, Straus & Giroux, 1979.

Longworth, David. *A Brief Narrative of the Trial for the Bloody and Mysterious Murder of the Unfortunate Young Woman in the Famous Manhattan Well.* Taken in Short Hand by a Gentleman of the Bar. New York, 1800.

————. *New York Register and City Directory for the Twenty-fifth Year of American Independence.* New York: D. Longworth, 1800.

Loth, David. *Alexander Hamilton, Portrait of a Prodigy.* New York: Carrick & Evans, Inc., 1939.

Lyman, Susan E. *The Story of New York.* New York: Crown Publishers, 1964.

Malone, Dumas, ed. *Dictionary of American Biography.* New York: Charles Scribner's Sons. Vol. 5, 1921, Vol. 6, 1933.

Mitchell, Broadus. *Alexander Hamilton: A Concise Biography.* New York: Oxford University Press, 1976.

————. *Alexander Hamilton, the National Adventure: 1788-1804.* 2 vols. New York: Macmillan Co., 1962.

Monaghan, Frank and Marvin Lowenthal. *This Was New York.* New York: Doubleday, Doran & Co., Inc., 1943.

Moore, Doris Langley. *The Child in Fashion.* London: B.T. Batsford, Ltd., 1953.

Morgan, Helen M., ed. *A Season in New York: 1801, Letters of Harriet and Maria Trumbull.* Pittsburgh: University of Pittsburgh Press, 1969.

Morris, Richard B. *Alexander Hamilton and the Founding of the Nation.* New York: Dial Press, 1957.

National Cyclopaedia of American Biography. Vol. 9. New York: James T. White & Co., 1907.

Nevins, Allan. *The Evening Post.* New York: Boni and Liveright, 1922.

Parmet, Herbert S. and Marie B. Hecht. *Aaron Burr, Portrait of an Ambitious Man.* New York: Macmillan Co., 1967.

Parton, James. *The Life and Times of Aaron Burr.* 1858. Reprint. New York: Johnson Reprint Corp., 1967.

Pomerantz, Sidney I. *New York, an American City: 1783-1803.* New York: Columbia University Press, 1938.

Ratner, Vivienne. "The Underground Railroad in Westchester" in *Westchester Historian* 59, 2 (Spring, 1983): 39-47.

Records of the Monthly Meeting of the Society of Friends. New York: Havilland Records Room.

Report of the Manhattan Company. New York: John Furman, 1799.

Report of the Trial of Richard D. Croucher on an Indictment for a Rape on Margaret Miller. People v. R.D. Croucher (8 July 1800), from Minutes of the Court of Oyer and Terminer and General Gaol Delivery, 1796-1801 (Readex Microfilm Evans 38373).

Roberts, Ellis H. *New York.* Boston: Houghton Mifflin Co., 1897.

Roberts, Kenneth and Anna M. Roberts, trans. and eds. *Moreau de St. Mery's American Journey: 1793-1798.* New York: Doubleday & Co., 1947.

Schachner, Nathan. *Aaron Burr.* New York: A.S. Barnes & Co., 1961.

Smith, Page. *John Adams.* 2 vols. New York: Doubleday & Co., 1962.

Smith, Sir Sidney. *Mostly Murder.* New York: David McKay Co., Inc., 1959.

Smith, Thomas E.V. *The City of New York in the Year of Washington's Inauguration.* 1889. Reprint. Riverside, Conn.: Chatham Press, 1972.

Stevens, William O. *Pistols at Ten Paces.* Boston: Houghton Mifflin, 1940.

Stokes, I.N. Phelps. *Iconography of Manhattan Island.* Vol. 5. 1926. Reprint. New York: Arno Press, 1967.

Story of the Old Homestead: 1732-1932. Cornwall, N.Y.: The Two Hundredth Anniversary Committee, 1932.

Tuni, Edwin. *The Young United States.* New York: Thos. Y. Crowell Co., 1969.

Valentine, David T. *Manuals of the Corporation of the City of New York.* New York, 1861.

Wandell, Samuel H. and Meade Minnigerode. *Aaron Burr.* New York: G.P. Putnam's Sons, 1927.

Willard, David. *History of Greenfield.* Greenfield, Mass.: Kneeland & Eastman, 1838.

Wilson, James Grant. *Memorial History of the City of New York.* Vol. 3. New York: New York History Co., 1893.

Wilson, Rufus Rockwell. *New York in Literature.* Elmira, N.Y.: Primavera Press, 1947.

INDEX

The following is an index of proper names only and does not include Elma Sands or Levi Weeks. The Manhattan Well and the names of the attorneys for the defense and the prosecution have not been listed when they appear within trial testimony, except in the case of major speeches.